Madame Alexander

Collector's Dolls
Price Guide

#19

Patricia R. Smith

COLLECTOR BOOKS
A Division of Schroeder Publishing Co., Inc.

Searching For A Publisher?

We are always looking for knowledgeable people considered to be experts within their fields. If you feel that there is a real need for a book on your collectible subject and have a large comprehensive collection, contact us.

COLLECTOR BOOKS
P.O. Box 3009
Paducah, Kentucky 42002-3009.

Additional copies of this book may be ordered from:

Collector Books
P.O. Box 3009
Paducah, Kentucky 42002-3009

@ $9.95 plus $2.00 for postage and handling.

Copyright: Patricia R. Smith, 1994

Printed by IMAGE GRAPHICS, INC., Paducah, Kentucky

Thank you ...

to Frances Stephens of Stone Mountain, Georgia for her five years of correspondence, information, and dedication to Madame Alexander dolls.

– Patricia R. Smith

— Madame Alexander Doll Club —

For membership information, write to:
Madame Alexander Doll Club (M.A.D.C.)
615 West 131st Street
New York, NY 10027.

PHOTO CREDITS

Gloria Anderson, Shirley Bertrand, Richard Boss, Lee Crane, Linda Crowsey, Jenni Ethell, Greg Ford, Frasher Doll Auctions, Gary Green, Barbara Henderson, Chris Johnson, Roger Jones, Floyd & Gracie James, Kris Lundquist, Marge Meisinger, Amy Merrill, Sharon McDowell, Margaret Mandel, Jeannie Mauldin, Pam Ortman, Flip & Florence Phelps, Peggy Pergande, Lia Sargent, David Spurgeon, Charmaine Shields, Martha Sweeny, Turn of Century Antiques, Glorya Woods, Mike Way, Janette Van Butiel.

Cover: 19" Madame Alexander, 1984. Courtesy Bill and Meredith Schroeder.

ABOUT PRICING

Prices in this guide are based upon a *perfect* doll. An exceptional doll will bring higher prices and a doll that is less than perfect should be priced lower than price given.

The question most often asked is, "What is a perfect doll?" *Perfect* refers to doll and clothes only, with the following items present and necessary to warrant the statement, "This doll is perfect."

1. Outfit correct and complete on correct doll.
2. Doll and clothes must be in overall excellent, perfect condition.
3. Original hair set, hair shiny and perfect.
4. Overall eye appeal that allows for a scale in pricing.
5. All items present, such as hats, shoes, dog, toys, etc.
6. Tagged clothing in original condition, including Madame Alexander undergarments.
7. Unblemished coloring to doll and clothes. Facial coloring to your liking.
8. Properly functioning mechanisms, if walker, jointed, etc.
9. No broken lashes or pulled hair lashes.
10. No stains, shelf dust, rips, fading, moth holes, tears, cut tags, missing clothing, missing snaps, pulled elastic.
11. Clothes have not been laundered or ironed.
12. Eyes open and close properly.
13. No chipped lips, missing paint or scratches.
14. No glue marks around face, no cracks in doll's seams.

An *exceptional* doll would be better than a *perfect* doll. The following list shows what could add a greater price to an already perfect doll:

1. Wrist Tag.
2. Box.
3. Original price tag.
4. Rare clothing, color variation or hairstyle.
5. Autographed.
6. Madame Alexander boxed items that originally sold separately, such as coats, hats, glasses, etc., and given to original doll.
7. Unique, pristine, "tissue mint."
8. With wardrobe, trunk or case.

A *less than perfect* doll would be one with any of the following, and priced lower according to how many defects are present.

1. Not original tagged clothes in perfect condition.
2. Stains, spots, soil, shelf dust, any discoloration or fading.
3. Tears, rips, cuts, missing snaps, pulled or re-stitched elastic.
4. No tag or cut tag.
5. Re-dressed dolls.
6. Washed or dry cleaned clothes.

7. Hair mussed up, dirty, cut, pulled out places.
8. Glue marks around face or discolored face.
9. Missing items such as shoes, socks, hats, etc.
10. Replaced items.
11. Broken or cracked parts on body, fingers, limbs or head.
12. Missing eyelashes, broken eyelids.
13. Washed out face color, no cheek color, eyebrow paint missing or changed color.
14. Clothes not on correct year doll.
15. Mechanisms, such as walker, not functioning correctly.

If a scale were made to show a perfect, exceptional and less than perfect doll, it would look like this:

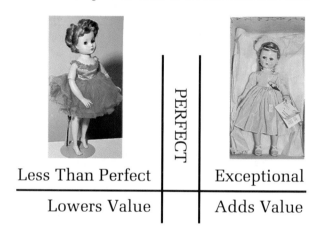

Less Than Perfect	PERFECT	Exceptional
Lowers Value		Adds Value

When buying Madame Alexander dolls, the main concern is *condition* of the doll and clothes. The Madame Alexander Doll Company designs fantastic clothes and the dolls are used to display clothes for a two-fold effect. One is artistic and the other is realistic, giving the full effect of doll and clothes for complete eye appeal. Therefore when purchasing a Madame Alexander doll, there must be perfect eye appeal to you, the buyer, along with a perfect doll and clothes.

There is no guarantee that *any* doll, antique or modern, will appreciate year after year. Prices remain high on exceptional dolls and always will. Much to the dismay of most of us, there always seems to be someone around who can and will spend the kind of money it takes to buy them. At times, the prices go higher on a plentiful perfect or exceptional doll due to the popularity of that particular doll.

What a person is willing to pay depends upon their financial resources and their willingness to spend. Because there are a great number of people who can and will spend large sums for a doll, it keeps the prices up, but not on all dolls, just on those particular ones. Since most people do have limited doll money, the rest of us want to be certain we are getting the most for our money.

There used to be new collectors who would buy less than perfect Madame Alexander dolls, but their ranks have slimmed down considerably. The majority of present day doll collectors want the best doll they can afford, with many willing to wait until they have the amount of funds available to buy one perfect Madame Alexander doll instead of several less than perfect ones. Collectors still buy for personal preference, individual eye appeal and think of investment in relation to the doll, with some buying for sentiment as it may have been the type of doll they had as a child or one their own children played with. No matter the reason, the most important factor is price versus condition. One more important reason for a purchase may be the collector's own need for their collection, such as to finish a certain set like the Sound of Music, Little Women, etc.

New collectors are being created each and every day by shoppers seeing and buying dolls from store shelves. Most of these people are totally unaware of "organized" doll collecting, such as clubs, publications, doll shows, etc. Starting in 1989, assistance has been provided for these beginners in the form of a card in each Alexander doll box, inviting them to join the Madame Alexander Doll Club (M.A.D.C.).

Collectors of "newer" Alexander dolls often branch out and begin buying older dolls through flea markets, shows and other secondary markets. These people should be aware of the following points:

1. Mold marks can be the same for an extended period of time. For example, 14" "Mary Ann" dolls will be marked "1965," which was the first year the doll was made. From then and until now, all "Mary Ann" face dolls will bear the 1965 mold number. Another example is the 21" "Jacqueline" doll, first introduced in 1961. Since 1965, all portraits have been based on the "Jacqueline" doll and bear the 1961 date. Determining the exact year any particular doll was made can be difficult for that reason.

2. Many times the Alexander Doll Company used the very same photographs to illustrate their catalogs, year after year. There are many variations of the same basic costume, especially in the 8" dolls and the only way an exact year for the particular doll can be found is in the booklet attached to the wrist of the doll. There can be, and are, many variations in costume during the year, depending on availability of colors and prints at the factory.

"Dealers" cannot pay price guide prices for dolls, as they must add expenses such as travel, booth rental, telephone calls, etc., and they must find a buyer, plus they must make a profit. The dealer has to consider all these things prior to making a purchase for resale. The dealer who is sensitive to the market realizes they must resell a doll based upon what they had to give for it, which depends upon the source they purchased from. Sometimes a dealer can resell below "book value," and at other times must get book values. Price guides are based on a doll being purchased from a dealer. A collector may search other sources to obtain dolls at lower prices, such as estate sales, ads in local papers, or by searching for dolls in out-of-the-way places. When discussing dealers, it must be noted that when dolls are purchased on a layaway plan versus cash, the layaway may be higher, but gives the collector the opportunity to own an exceptional doll.

Price guides must be based upon prices for a *perfect* doll and all collectors need accurate prices for insurance reasons. An insurance company or a postal service must have some means to appraise a damaged or stolen doll for the insuree, and the collector must have some means to judge their own collections to be able to purchase adequate amounts of insurance.

A price guide is a *guide* and not the "last word," as we ourselves have the "last word" in our own dealings. We do not have to pay an asking price unless we want the doll and can afford it.

Madame Alexander dolls will always be collectible and endure time and value. Beautiful dolls have flowed from this factory for over 65 years and will continue to do so. We hope all of you will continue to build the collections you so desire, be they older dolls or the excellent current dolls that become available each year.

Abbreviations are:
    hp – hard plastic
    Compo – composition
    C.U. – Collector United Newspaper
    F.A.D. – factory altered outfit
    SLNW – straight leg, non-walker
    SLW – straight leg walker
    BKW – bend knee walker
    BK – bend knee
    U.F.D.C. – United Federation of Doll Clubs
    M.A.D.C. - Madame Alexander Doll Club

The dolls named after real people are listed with last name first (Example: "Bliss, Betty Taylor"). Make-believe doll names will be listed with first name first (Example: "Tommy Snooks").

Some 8" International, Storybook Dolls, 21" Portraits, 10" Portrettes, babies, and 14" dolls are selling below suggested retail/catalog prices. There are over 270 different 8" Storybook, Internations, and Americana dolls plus variations of materials or colors used. Dolls order/box numbers for 8" dolls with "0" prefix (example: 0742) were used in 1973 only. It must be noted the box/order numbers found with doll's name are from Alexander catalogs, but many dolls were placed in wrong boxes by the stores from which they were sold.

THE MANY FACES OF MADAME ALEXANDER DOLLS

WENDY ANN (COMPO.)

TINY & LITTLE BETTY

PRINCESS ELIZABETH

MAGGIE

MARGARET (O'BRIEN)

CISSY

ELISE (1950's – 1960's)

LISSY

CISSETTE

MARY-BEL

JACQUELINE

MARY ANN

ELISE (1960's – 1980's)

POLLY & LESLIE

NANCY DREW

WENDY ANN – NEW 1988 FACE

MAGGIE MIXUP (1960–1961)

MAGGIE MIXUP (1988–1991)

Please read "About Pricing" for additional information.

ACTIVE MISS 18" hp., 1954 only, (Violet/Cissy) 550.00
ADAMS, ABIGAIL 1976–1978, Presidents' Ladies/First Ladies Series, First Set (Mary Ann)................110.00
ADAMS, LOUISA 1976–1978, Presidents' Ladies/First Ladies Series, First Set (Louisa) 110.00
AFRICA 8" hp., #766, 1966–1971, BK (Wendy Ann) 275.00
    8" hp. straight leg re-issued, #523–583, 1988–1992, (Wendy Ann) 52.00
AGATHA 18" hp. (Cissy)
    1954 only, Me and My Shadow Series, rose taffeta dress ....850.00 up
    8" hp. (Wendy Ann), #00308, 1953–1954, black top and floral gown ....1,200.00 up
    21" Portrait, #2171, 1967, red gown (Jacqueline) 650.00
        #2297, 1974, pink gown with full length cape (Jacqueline).................................500.00
        #2291, 1975, blue with white sequin trim (Jacqueline) 475.00
        #2294, 1976, blue with white rick-rack trim (Jacqueline)................................400.00
        #2230, 1979, 1980, 1981, lavender 325.00
        #2230, 1981, blue (Jacqueline) 295.00
    10" Portrette, #1171, 1968 only, red velvet (Cissette) 450.00
AGNES Cloth/felt, 1930's 650.00
ALADDIN 8" hp., #482, 1993, Storybook Series 55.00
ALASKA 8", #302, 1990–1992, Americana Series (Maggie) 56.00
ALBANIA 8" straight leg, #526, 1987 only (Wendy Ann) 60.00
ALEXANDER RAG TIME DOLLS Cloth, 1938–1939 only ....800.00 up
ALEXANDER-KINS 7½–8" hp., must have good face color (Wendy Ann)
If doll is not listed here, see regular listing for name. (Add more for mint or mint in box dolls. Special hairdos are higher priced.)

Straight leg non-walker, 1953–1954. (First price is for 1953 strung doll.)	**Mint**	
Coat/hat (dress)	425.00	325.00
Cotton dress/organdy pinafore	475.00	350.00
Cotton dress/cotton pinafore	475.00	350.00
Day in Country long gown	1,000.00	
Dresser/doll/wardrobe	2,000.00 up	
Easter doll	900.00	
Felt jackets/pleated skirt dresses	575.00	
Garden Party long gown	1,100.00 up	
Jumper/one-piece bodysuit	250.00	200.00
Nightgown	250.00	200.00
Nude/perfect doll (Excellent face color)	200.00	125.00
Organdy dress/cotton pinafore/hat	600.00	450.00
Organdy dress/organdy pinafore/hat	600.00	450.00
Satin dress/cotton pinafore/hat	575.00	450.00
Satin dress/organdy pinafore/hat	575.00	450.00
Sleeveless satin/organdy or cotton pinafore	425.00	325.00
Robe/nightgown or P.J.'s	325.00	225.00
Taffeta dress/cotton pinafore/hat	575.00	450.00

Straight leg walker, 1955 only, must have good face color. (Add more for mint or mint in box dolls.)
    Basic doll in box/panties/shoes/socks 250.00
    Coat/hat (dress)..325.00
    Cotton dress/pinafore 260.00
    Cotton school dress 250.00
    Garden Party long gown ....1,000.00 up
    Nude/perfect doll (Excellent face color) 175.00
    Maypole Dance 400.00
    Nightgown 150.00

Organdy party dress/hat 450.00
P.J.'s 150.00
Riding Habit ....385.00 up
Robe/nightgown or P.J.'s 145.00
Sailor dress 800.00
Sleeveless organdy dress 250.00
Swimsuits 225.00
Taffeta/satin party dress/hat 425.00
Bend knee walker, 1956–1964, must have good face color. (Add more for mint or mint in box dolls.)
Nude (Excellent face color) 125.00
Basic doll in box/panties/shoes/socks 250.00
Carcoat set 475.00
Cherry Twin (each)..1,200.00 up
Coat/hat 200.00
Cotton dress/cotton pinafore...250.00
Cotton or satin dress/organdy pinafore/hat ....300.00 up
First Dancing dress (gown) 650.00
Felt jacket/pleated skirt/dress/cap or hat 350.00
Flowergirl ....1,200.00 up
June Wedding 775.00
Long party dress ....1,000.00 up
Taffeta party dress/hat..375.00
Nightgown/robe 175.00
Neiman-Marcus in case/all clothes (*Must be on correct doll/hairdo) 950.00
　*Name of store printed on material 650.00
　*2 pc. playsuit 375.00
　*Robe 175.00

**8" Wendy-Alexander-kin, bend knee, 1956. Furniture from same period.
Mint and above book price. Set valued at $350.00.**

Organdy dress/organdy pinafore/hat 350.00
Riding habit, corduroy, girl 400.00
  Riding habit, boy 425.00
  Devon Horse Show 600.00
Skater 475.00
Sleeveless school dress 225.00
Sundress 225.00
Swimsuits, beach outfits 200.00
Velvet party dress 850.00
Bend Knee, non-walkers, 1965–1972. (Add more for mint or mint in box dolls.)
  Basic doll in box with panties/shoes/socks 100.00
  Cotton dress, 1965 ....125.00
  Easter Egg/doll...1,500.00 up
  French Braid/cotton dress, 1965 ....200.00
  Felt jacket/skirt/dress/cap/hat, 1965 ....275.00 up
  Nude, perfect doll with excellent face color 60.00
  Organdy dress/hat, 1965 ....225.00
  Riding habit, check pants, girl, 1965 ....275.00
  Riding habit, check pants, boy, 1965 ....325.00
  Sewing kit/doll ....1,400.00 up
ALICE 18" hp., 1951 only (Maggie) 775.00
ALICE AND HER PARTY KIT 1965 only, included case, wardrobe and wigs (Mary Ann) ....750.00 up
ALICE IN WONDERLAND
  16" cloth, 1930 and 1933 ....600.00
  7" compo., 1930's (Tiny Betty) 245.00
  9" compo., 1930's (Little Betty) 325.00

**8" WENDY-ALEXANDER-KIN,
bend knee, 1956.
Exceptional doll, above book price.**

ALICE IN WONDERLAND.
**18" composition from 1948; 21" hard plastic
from 1949; 18" hard plastic from 1951.**

11–14" compo., 1936–1940 (Wendy Ann) 450.00

13" compo., 1930's, has swivel waist (Wendy Ann) 450.00

14½–18" compo., 1948–1949 (Margaret) 550.00

21" compo., 1948–1949 (Margaret) 950.00

15", 18", 21" compo., 1930's (Wendy Ann) 425.00–750.00

14½" hp., 1949–1950 (Margaret) 600.00

14" hp., 1950 (Maggie) 650.00

17–23" hp. 1949–1950 (Maggie & Margaret) ....625.00–800.00 up

15", 18", 23" hp., 1951–1952 (Maggie & Margaret) ....500.00, 600.00, 800.00 up

14" hp. with trousseau, 1951–1952 (Maggie) ....1,300.00 up

29" cloth/vinyl, 1952 (Barbara Jane) ....500.00 up

29" vinyl, 1952 (Annabelle) ....575.00 up

8" hp., #465–#590, 1955–1956 (Wendy Ann) 650.00

8", #494, Storyland Series, blue/white eyelet pinafore 52.00

    #492, 1993–, blue/white with red trim 52.00

12", 1963 (Lissy) 1,000.00

14" plastic/vinyl, #1452 to 1974, #1552, 1966–1992, Literature & Classic Series (Mary Ann)......74.00

8" hp., 1972–1976, Disney Crest Color, (Disneyland, Disney World) 450.00

10", 1991, with white rabbit (see Disney under Special Events/Exclusives)

ALCOTT, LOUISA MAY 14", #1529, 1989–1990, Classic Series (Mary Ann) 80.00

    8" hp., #409, 1992 only, Storyland Series (Wendy Ann) 57.00

ALGERIA 8" straight leg, #528, 1988 only (Maggie) 58.00

ALL STAR 8" hp., #346–346-1, Americana Series, white or black......................................60.00

ALLISON 18" cloth/vinyl, 1990–1991 only 100.00

ALPINE BOY AND GIRL 1992 (see Christmas Shoppe under Special Events/Exclusives)

ALTAR BOY 8" hp., #311, 1991 only, Americana Series 60.00

AMANDA 8" hp., #489, 1961 only, Americana Series, burnt orange/lace trim (Wendy Ann)....2,200.00 up

AMERICAN BABIES 16–18" cloth, 1930's..250.00–345.00

AMERICAN BEAUTY 10" Portrette, #1142, 1991–1992 only, all pink 80.00

AMERICAN GIRL 7–8" compo., 1938 (Tiny Betty) 225.00

    9–11" compo., 1937 (Little Betty, Wendy Ann) 275.00–450.00

    8" hp., #388, #788, 1962–1963, became "McGuffey Ana" in 1964–1965, (Wendy Ann).............375.00

AMERICAN INDIAN 9" compo., 1938–1939 (Little Betty) 275.00

AMERICAN TOTS 16–21" cloth, dressed in child's fashions. 275.00–450.00

AMERICAN WOMEN'S VOLUNTEER SERVICE (AWVS) 14" compo., 1942 (Wendy Ann) 800.00

AMISH BOY 8" hp., BK, #727, 1966–1969, Americana Series (Wendy Ann) 400.00

AMISH GIRL 8" hp. BK, #726, 1966–1969, Americana Series (Wendy Ann) 400.00

AMY (see "Little Women").

ANASTASIA 10" Portrette, #1125, 1988–1989 (Cissette) 78.00

ANATOLIA 8" straight leg, #524, 1987 only 52.00

ANGEL 8", in pink, blue, off-white gowns (Wendy & Maggie) 975.00

    8" Guardian, #480, 1954 only, (Wendy Ann) 950.00

    8" Guardian, #618, 1961 (Maggie Mixup) 985.00

    8" hp. Baby, #480, 1955, multi-layered chiffon wings (Wendy Ann)........................985.00

ANGEL FACE 8" (see "Special Events/Exclusives")

ANGEL TREE TOPPER (see "Tree Topper")

ANNA BALLERINA 18" compo., 1940, Pavlova (Wendy Ann) ....1,200.00 up

ANNABELLE 14–15" hp., 1951–1952 only (Maggie) 475.00

    14–15" trousseau/trunk, 1952 only...1,200.00 up

    18" hp., 1951–1952 ....600.00

    20–23" hp., 1951–1952 ....650.00–725.00

ANNABELLE AT CHRISTMAS (see Belks under Special Events/Exclusives)

ANNA KARENINA 21" Portrait, #2265, 1991 (Jacqueline) 340.00

ANNE OF GREEN GABLES 14", #1530, 1989–1990 only (Mary Ann) 110.00
  14", #1579, reintroduced 1992–1993, with trunk/wardrobe (Louisa/Jennifer) 260.00
  14", #1570, 1992–1993, Arrives At Station 145.00
    1992–1993, white organdy dress only..52.00
    1992–1993, puff sleeve dress only 42.00
    1992–1993, winter coat outfit only 52.00
    1993, Becomes The Teacher 155.00
ANNIE LAURIE 14" compo., 1937 (Wendy Ann) 700.00
  17" compo., 1937 (Wendy Ann) 875.00
ANTOINETTE 21" compo., 1946 (Wendy Ann) 2,200.00
ANTOINE, MARIE 21", 1987–1988 only, multi-floral with pink front insert (Wendy Ann)..................600.00
ANTONY, MARK 12", #1310, 1980–1985, Portraits of History (Nancy Drew) 50.00
APPLE ANNIE OF BROADWAY 8" hp., 1953–1954 (Wendy Ann) ....1,250.00 up
APPLE PIE 14", #1542, 1991 only, Classics (Mary Ann)................................87.00
APRIL 14", #1533, 1990–1991, Doll Classics (Mary Ann & Jennifer)....................95.00
ARGENTINE BOY 8" hp., BKW & BK, #772, 1965 only (Wendy Ann) 385.00
ARGENTINE GIRL 8" hp., BK, #0771-571, 1965–1972 (Wendy Ann)....................125.00
  BKW, #771 (Wendy Ann) 175.00
  8" hp., straight legs, #571, 1973–1976, marked "Alex" 62.00
  8" hp., straight legs, #571, 1976–1986 (1985–1986 white face) 55.00
ARMENIA 8", #507, 1989–1990 (Wendy Ann) 52.00
ARRIVING IN AMERICA 8" hp., #326, 1992–1993, Americana Series (Wendy Ann) 55.00

8" ARGENTINE BOY. 1965 only.

ARTIE 12" plastic/vinyl, 1962, sold through FAO Schwarz (Smarty) 300.00
ASHLEY 8", #628, 1990 only, Scarlett Series, tan jacket/hat 72.00
   8" hp., #633, 1991–1992 only, Scarlett Series, as Confederate officer 65.00
ASTOR 9" early vinyl toddler, 1953 only, gold organdy dress & bonnet...100.00
ASTROLOGICAL MONTH DOLLS 14–17" compo., 1938 (Wendy) 550.00
AUNT AGATHA 8" hp., #434, 1957 (Wendy Ann)..1,200.00 up
AUNT BETSY Cloth/felt, 1930's 650.00
AUNT PITTY PAT 14–17" compo., 1939 (Wendy Ann)...1,200.00–1,850.00 up
   8" hp., #435, 1957 (Wendy Ann)...1,600.00 up
   8" hp., straight leg, #636, 1991–1992, Scarlett Series 57.00
AUSTRALIA 8", #504, 1990–1991 only (Wendy Ann) 58.00
AUSTRIA BOY* 8" hp., 1974–1989 (Wendy Ann)
   Straight legs, #599–#533, 1973–1975, marked "Alex" 60.00
   #599, 1976–1989, marked "Alexander" (1985–1987 white face) 55.00
AUSTRIA GIRL* 8" hp., 1974–1993 (Wendy Ann)
   Straight legs, #598, 1973–1975, marked "Alex."..60.00
   #598–#532, 1976–1990, marked "Alexander" (1985–1987 white face) 55.00
AUTUMN 14", 1993, Changing Seasons Doll with four outfits 145.00
AUTUMN IN N.Y. (see first Modern Doll Club under "Special Events/Exclusives")
AVRIL, JANE 10" (see "Special Events/Exclusives")

* *Formerly* TYROLEAN BOY AND GIRL

Please read "About Pricing" for additional information.

Babbie Cloth with long thin legs, inspired by Katherine Hepburn. ....700.00 up
    16", cloth child doll, 1934–1936 ....500.00 up
    14" hp. (Maggie) ....575.00 up
Babs 20" hp., 1949 (Maggie) 650.00
Babs Skater 15" hp., 1948–1950 (Margaret) 500.00
    17–18" hp. 600.00
    21" hp. 700.00
    18" compo. (Margaret) 625.00
Babette 10" Portrette, #1117, 1988–1989 (Cissette), black short dress 78.00
Babsie Baby Compo./cloth, moving tongue 475.00
Babsie Skater (roller) 15", 1941 (Princess Elizabeth) ....600.00 up
Baby Betty 10–12" compo., 1935–1936 ....250.00
Baby Brother and Sister 20", cloth/vinyl, 1977–1979 (Mary Mine) ....80.00 each
    14", 1979–1982 ....65.00 each
    14", re-introduced 1989 only ....60.00 each
Baby Clown 8" hp., #464, 1955, has painted face (Wendy Ann) ....1,500.00 up
Baby Ellen 14", 1965–1972 (black "Sweet Tears") 85.00
Baby Genius 11" all cloth, 1930's 475.00
    11–12" compo./cloth, 1930's–1940's ....150.00 up
    16" compo./cloth, 1930's–1940's 175.00
    15", 18", 21" hp. head, vinyl limbs, 1949–1950 ....80.00–145.00
    8" hp./vinyl, 1956–1962 (see Little Genius)
Baby Jane 16" compo., 1935 ....900.00 up
Baby Lynn 20" cloth/vinyl, 1973–1976 ....125.00
    14" cloth/vinyl, 1973–1976 ....100.00 (mint - 225.00)

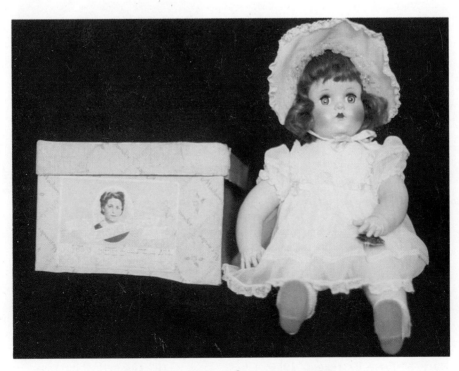

16" Baby Genius from 1949–1950.
Above book price because of condition.

BABY MCGUFFEY 22–24" compo., 1937 ....185.00
    20" cloth/vinyl, 1971–1976 ....125.00
    14" cloth/vinyl, 1972–1978 ....100.00
BABY PRECIOUS 14" cloth/vinyl, 1975 only ....65.00 up
    21" cloth/vinyl, 1974–discontinued 1976 ....92.00
BABY IN LOUIS VUITTON TRUNK/WARDROBE Any year ....750.00 up
BABY SHAVER 12–13" hp., 1941–1943 (same face),
    red mohair hair, long blue, pink, or lavendar gown, cap and booties ....450.00 up
BAD LITTLE GIRL 16" cloth, 1966 only, blue dress, eyes and mouth turned down, looking sad.......185.00
BALI 8" hp., #533, 1993 ....54.00
BALLERINA (Also see individual dolls – Leslie, Margaret, etc.)
    9" compo., 1935–1941 (Little Betty) 300.00
    11–13", 1930's (Betty) 250.00–350.00
    11–14" compo., 1936–1938 (Wendy Ann) 275.00–300.00
    17" compo., 1938–1941 (Wendy Ann) ....600.00 up
    21" compo., 1947, "Deborah" ("Debra") Portrait ballerina in mint condition (Wendy Ann) 2,600.00
    8" hp., must have excellent face color. (Wendy Ann)
        SLNW, #354, 1953–1954, lavender, yellow, or pink 575.00
            Blue 575.00
        SLW, #454, 1955, lavender, yellow, pink, or white 565.00
            #454, blue 525.00
    BKW, #564, 1954–1960, golden yellow 525.00
        #364, 1957, blue 450.00
        #564, 1956, rose 550.00
        #420, 1961, lavender 600.00

Rare 8" ROSE BALLERINA, 1956.
Price above average due to condition.

10" CISSETTE BALLERINA,
1957–1959.

B

        #420, 1959, gold 575.00
        #544, 1958, pink 250.00
        #564–631, 1956, yellow 500.00
        #454, 1955, white 425.00
        #640, 1964, white 385.00
    BK, #620-730, 1965–1972, yellow 375.00
        #440-730, 1962–1972, blue 250.00
        #440-730, 1962–1972, pink 200.00
    8" straight leg, #0730, #530, #430, 1973–1992 (1985–1987 white face) 60.00
    8" Enchanted Doll House (see Special Events/Exclusive)
    8", #330, 1990–1991 (black or white dolls, 1991), Americana Series, white/gold outfit (Wendy Ann) ...65.00
        #331–331-1, 1992, black or white doll in pink/silver outfit (Wendy Ann) 52.00
        #331, 1993, white doll only pink/silver outfit 52.00
    8", 1984 (see M.A.D.C. under Special Events/Exclusives)
    10–11" hp., 1957–1959, must have excellent face color (Cissette)...............................450.00
    12", 1964 only (Janie) 325.00
    12", 1989–1990, "Muffin," (Janie) 70.00
    12", 1990–1992 only, Romance Collection (Nancy Drew) 72.00
    12", 1993, in lavendar (Lissy)..102.00
    14" hp., 1956 (15" & 18", 1956 only) (Binnie, Cissy) 300.00
    14", 1963 only (Melinda) ....400.00 up
    15–18" hp., 1950–1952, must have good face color (Margaret) 450.00–600.00
    16½" hp., 1957, 1958, 1959, 1962 (Elise) 225.00
        1963 only (Marybel) (18" also Elise) 375.00
    17" plastic/vinyl, 1967–1989, discontinued costume (Elise)..100.00
    17" plastic/vinyl, 1990–1991, "Firebird" and "Swan Lake" (Elise) 135.00
    17", 1970–1971 only (Leslie)..325.00
BARBARA JANE 29" cloth/vinyl, 1952 only, mint 500.00
BARBARA LEE 8", 1955, name given by FAO Schwarz ....NPA
BARBARY COAST 10" hp., 1962–1963, Portrette Series, (Cissette)...........................1,200.00 up
BARTON, CLARA 10", #1130, 1989 only, Portrette Series, wears nurse's outfit (Cissette) 78.00
BEAU ART DOLLS 18" hp., 1953 only (Margaret, Maggie) ....1,200.00 up
BEAU BRUMMEL Cloth, 1930's...650.00
BEAUTY 12", 1992 only, Romance Series (Nancy Drew) 105.00
BEAST 12", 1992 only, Romance Series (Nancy Drew) 115.00
BEAUTY QUEEN 10" hp., 1961 only (Cissette) 235.00
BEDDY BYE BROOKE (see FAO Schwarz under Special Events/Exclusives)
BELGIUM 8" hp., BK, #762, 1972 only (Wendy Ann) 125.00
    8" straight legs, #0762, #562, 1973–1975, marked "Alex"...60.00
    8" straight legs, #562, 1976–1988, marked "Alexander" (1985–1987 white face) 55.00
    7" compo., 1935–1938 (Tiny Betty) 225.00
BELLE BRUMMEL Cloth, 1930's...650.00
BELLE OF THE BALL 10", #1120, 1989 only, Portrette Series, deep rose gown (Cissette) 78.00
BELLOWS' ANNE 14" plastic/vinyl, #1568, 1987 only, Fine Arts Series 80.00
BELK DEPARTMENT STORES (see Special Events/Exclusives)
BELLE WATLING 10", 1992 only, Scarlett Series (Cissette) 92.00
BERNHARDT, SARAH 21", #2249, 1987 only, dressed in all burgundy 325.00
BESSY BELL 14" plastic/vinyl, #1565, 1988 only, Classic Series (Mary Ann) 75.00
BESSY BROOKS 8", #487, 1988–1991, Storybook Series (Wendy Ann).............................60.00
    8", 1990 (see C.U. Gathering under Special Events/Exclusives)
BEST MAN 8" hp., #461, 1955 only (Wendy Ann) 750.00
BETH (see "Little Women")
    10" (see Spiegel's under Special Events/Exclusives) (Cissette)

BETTY   14" compo., 1935–1942 ....350.00

    12" compo., 1936–1937 only 500.00

    16–18" compo., 1935–1942 ....375.00–425.00

    19–21" compo., 1938–1941 ....375.00–500.00

    14½–17½" hp., 1951 only, made for Sears (Maggie) 500.00–600.00

    30" plastic/vinyl, 1960 only 400.00

BETTY, TINY   7" compo., 1934–1943 ....250.00

BETTY, LITTLE   9" compo, 1935–1943 ....295.00

BETTY BAG   All cloth with flat painted face and yarn hair, 1940's 300.00

BETTY BLUE   8" straight leg, #420, 1987–1988 only, Storybook Series (Maggie) 60.00

BIBLE CHARACTER DOLLS   8" hp., 1954 (Wendy Ann) ....each   5,200.00 up

BILL/BILLY   8" hp., #320, #567, #420, 1955–1963, has boy's clothes and hair style (Wendy Ann) ...385.00

    #577, 464, #466, #421, #442, #488, #388, 1953–1957, as groom ....500.00 up

BINNIE   18" plastic/vinyl toddler, 1964 only 365.00

BINNIE WALKER   15–18" hp., 1954–1955 only (Cissy) 165.00–250.00

    15", 1955 only, in trunks/wardrobe 600.00

    15" hp. skater, 1955 only 325.00

    25" Informals, 1955 only 475.00

    25" hp., 1954–1955 only, dresses 325.00–375.00

BIRTHDAY DOLLS   7" compo., 1937–1939 (Tiny Betty) 350.00

BIRTHDAY, HAPPY   1985 (see M.A.D.C. under Special Events/Exclusives)

BITSEY   11–12" compo., 1942–1946 ....125.00

    11–16" with hp. head, 1949–1951 ....70.00–95.00

    19–26", 1949–1951 ....125.00–145.00

    12" cloth/vinyl, 1965–1966 only 75.00

8" BILL and WENDY in riding habits, 1957.

8" BLUE MOON, 1991–1992.

BITSEY, LITTLE 9" all vinyl, 1967–1968 only 85.00
  11–16" 30.00–150.00
BLACK FOREST 8", #512, 1989–1990 (Wendy Ann) 52.00
BLISS, BETTY TAYLOR 1979–1981, 2nd set First Ladies/Presidents' Ladies Series (Mary Ann).............90.00
BLUE BOY 16" cloth, 1930's 675.00
  7" compo., 1936–1938 (Tiny Betty) 265.00
  9" compo., 1938–1941 (Little Betty) 285.00
  12" plastic/vinyl, #1340, 1972–1983, Portrait Children (Nancy Drew) 60.00
  1985–1987, dressed in blue velvet 65.00
BLUE DANUBE 18" hp., 1953 only, pink floral gown (Margaret)............................1,400.00 up
  18" hp., 1954 only, Me and My Shadow Series, blue taffeta dress (Margaret) ....1,200.00 up
BLUE FAIRIE 10", #1166, Portrette Series, character from Pinocchio (Cissette) 92.00
BLUE MOON 14", #1560, 1991–1992 only, Classic Series (Louisa) 170.00
BLUE ZIRCON 10", #1153, 1992 only, Birthday Collection, gold/blue flapper 64.00
BLYNKINS (see "Dutch Lullaby.")
BOBBY 8" hp., #347, 1957 only (Wendy Ann) 475.00
  8" hp., #361, #320, 1960 only (Maggie Mixup) 500.00
BOBBY Q. Cloth, 1940–1942 ....650.00
BOBBY SOXER 8" hp., 1990–1991 (see Disney under Special Events/Exclusives)
BOBO CLOWN 8", #320, 1991–1992, Americana Series (Wendy Ann) 52.00
BOHEMIA 8", #508, 1989–1991 (Wendy Ann) 55.00
BOLIVIA 8" hp., BK & BKW, #786, 1963–1966 (Wendy Ann) 475.00
BONNIE (BABY) 16–19" vinyl, 1954–1955 ....65.00
  24–30", 1954–1955 ....125.00–150.00
BONNIE BLUE 14", #1305, 1989 only, Jubilee II (Mary Ann) 120.00
  8" hp., #629, #630, 1990–1992 (Wendy Ann) 57.00
  8", (see Dolly Dears under Special Events/Exclusives)
BONNIE GOES TO LONDON 8", #640, 1993, Scarlett Series 65.00
BONNIE TODDLER 18" cloth/hp. head/vinyl limbs, 1950–1951 ....95.00
  19" all vinyl, 1954–1955 ....125.00
  23–24" 165.00
BOONE, DANIEL 8" hp., #315, 1991 only, Americana Series, has no knife (Wendy Ann) 60.00
BO PEEP, LITTLE 7" compo., 1937–1941, Storybook Series (Tiny Betty)................250.00
  9–11" compo., 1936–1940 (Little Betty, Wendy Ann) 285.00–350.00
  7½" hp., SLW, #489, 1955 only (Wendy Ann) 500.00
  8" hp., BKW, #383, 1962–1964 (Wendy Ann) 365.00
  8" hp., BK, #783, 1965–1972 (Wendy Ann) 135.00
  8" hp., straight leg, #0783-483, 1973–1975, marked "Alex" (Wendy Ann)..............60.00
  8" hp., 1976–1986, #483–#486, marked "Alexander" (1985–1986 white face) (Wendy Ann) 55.00
  14", #1563, 1988–1989, Classic Series (Mary Ann)..70.00
  14", #1567, reintroduced 1992–1993, candy stripe pink dress (Mary Ann)............130.00
  12" porcelain, #009, 1990–1992 ....265.00
  8" (see Dolly Dears under Special Events/Exclusives)
BRAZIL 7" compo., 1937–1943 (Tiny Betty) 225.00
  9" compo., 1938–1940 (Little Betty) 265.00
  8" hp., BKW, #773, 1965–1972 (Wendy Ann) 225.00
  BK, #773 ....125.00
  8" hp., straight leg, #0773, #573, 1973–1975, marked "Alex." (Wendy Ann) 60.00
  8" hp., straight leg, #573, #547, #530, 1976–1988, marked "Alexander" (1985–1987 white face)...55.00
  #573, #547, #530, 1985–1987, white face 50.00
BRENDA STARR 12" hp., 1964 only (became "Yolanda" in 1965) 225.00
  Bride 250.00
  Street dresses 225.00

Ball gown 300.00
Beach outfit 200.00
Raincoat/hat/dress 250.00
BRIAR ROSE 8" (see M.A.D.C. under Special Events/Exclusives)
BRIDE 7" compo., 1935–1939 (Tiny Betty)...225.00
   9–11" compo., 1936–1941 (Little Betty) 250.00–300.00
   13", 14", 15" compo., 1935–1941 (Wendy Ann)..................................275.00–325.00
   17–18" compo., 1935–1943 (Wendy Ann) 425.00
   21–22" compo., 1942–1943 (Wendy Ann) ....600.00 up
     In trunk/trousseau (Wendy Ann) ....1,500.00 up
   21" compo., 1945–1947, Royal Wedding/Portrait ....2,400.00 up
   15" hp., 1951–1955 (Margaret)...550.00
   17" hp., 1950, in pink (Margaret) 625.00
   18" hp., tagged "Prin. Elizabeth" (Margaret).......................................550.00
   18" hp., 1949–1955 (Maggie, Margaret)..600.00
   21" hp., 1949–1953 (Margaret, Maggie) 575.00

7" TINY BETTY BRIDE, 1935–1939.

23" hp. 1949, 1952–1955 (Margaret) 685.00
25" hp., 1955 only (Margaret) 700.00
16½" hp. 1957–1964 (18" in 1963 only), must have good face color (Elise) 350.00
20" hp., 1955–1958 (Cissy)
    1955 only, Dreams Come True Series, brocade gown with floor length veil 500.00
    1956 only, tulle gown, tulle cap & chapel length veil 475.00
    1957 only, Models Formal Gowns Series, nylon tulle with double train of satin 500.00
    1958 only, Dolls To Remember Series, lace circles near hem 575.00
10" hp., 1957–1963 (Cissette) 265.00
10" hp., various years, in trunk/trousseau (Cissette) ....900.00 up
10", #1136, 1990–1991, Portrette Series (Cissette) 85.00
12" hp., 1956–1959 (Lissy) 275.00
12" porcelain, 1991–1992 only, (version of 14" head) 255.00
21" Portrait, #2151, 1965, full lace, wide lace edge on veil (Jacqueline) ....900.00 up
    #2192, 1969, full lace overskirt and plain veil 800.00
8" hp., #315, 1953 only, Quizkin (Wendy Ann) 525.00
    SLW, BKW, #735 in 1955, #615 in 1956, #410 in 1957; #582 in 1958 ....350.00
    BKW, #482, 1959 ....250.00
    BKW, #735, 1960 ....300.00
    BKW, #480, 1961 ....250.00
    BKW, #760 (#630 in 1965), 1963–1965 ....250.00
    BK, #470 in 1966; #735 in 1967–1972 ....125.00
    Straight leg, #0735-435, 1973–1975, marked "Alex." 60.00
    Straight leg, #435, 1976–1993, marked "Alexander" 72.00
    #337, white doll; #336-1, black doll, 1991–1992 ....60.00
    #337, 1993, white only 60.00
    #435, 1985–1987, white face 50.00
8", factory altered for C.U. (see Special Events/Exclusives)
14" plastic/vinyl, #1465 (#1565 in 1974, #1565 in 1977, #1570 in 1976), 1973–1977 (Mary Ann) ..80.00
14" plastic/vinyl, (#1589 in 1987–1988; #1534 in 1990), 1987–1990,
    Classic Series (Mary Ann, Jennifer) 95.00
14", #1566, reintroduced 1992 only, ecru gown (Louisa, Jennifer) 165.00
17" plastic/vinyl, 1966–1988 (Elise) 145.00
17" plastic/vinyl, 1966–1971 (Leslie) 265.00
17" plastic/vinyl, 1965–1970 (Polly) 325.00
21" porcelain, 1989–1990, satin and lace look like bustle in front 520.00
Bridesmaid 9" compo., 1937–1939 (Little Betty) 245.00
11–14" compo., 1938–1942 (Wendy Ann) 265.00–425.00
15–18" compo., 1939–1944 (Wendy Ann) 450.00–575.00
20–22" compo., 1941–1947, Portrait (Wendy Ann) 2,200.00
21½" compo., 1938–1941 (Prin. Elizabeth) 950.00
15–17" hp., 1950–1952 (Margaret, Maggie) 425.00–575.00
15" hp., 1952 (Maggie) 450.00
18" hp., 1952 (Maggie) 625.00
21" hp., 1950–1953, side part mohair wig, deep pink or lavender gown (Margaret) 650.00
19" rigid vinyl, in pink, 1952–1953 (Margaret) 500.00
15" hp., 1955 only (Cissy, Binnie) 300.00
18" hp., 1955 only (Cissy, Binnie) 375.00
25" hp., 1955 only (Cissy, Binnie) 500.00
20" hp., 1956 only, Fashion Parade Series, blue nylon tulle & net (Cissy) 550.00
10" hp., 1957–1963 (Cissette) 450.00
12" hp., 1956–1959 (Lissy) 425.00
16½" hp., 1957–1959 (Elise) 425.00

8" hp., SLW, #478, 1955 (Wendy Ann) 650.00
    BKW, #621, 1956 ....575.00
    BKW, #408, #583, #445, 1957–1959 ....575.00
  17" (see Formals: Elise)
  17" plastic/vinyl, 1966–1971 (Leslie) 250.00
BRIGITTA 11" & 14" (see "Sound of Music") (Cissette, Mary Ann)
BROOKE 14", 1989 (see FAO Schwarz under Special Event/Exclusive)
BUBBLES CLOWN 8" hp., #342, 1993, Americana Series 55.00
BUCK RABBIT Cloth/felt, 1930's 600.00
BUD 16–19" cloth/vinyl, 1952 only (Rosebud head) 85.00
  19" & 25", 1952–1953 only 125.00–150.00
BULGARIA 8", #557, 1986–1987, white face (Wendy Ann) 55.00
BUMBLE BEE 8" hp., #323, 1992–1993, Americana Series 56.00
BUNNY 18" plastic/vinyl, 1962 only, mint 300.00
BURMA 7" compo., 1939–1943 (Tiny Betty) 300.00
BUTCH 11–12" compo./cloth, 1942–1946 ....125.00
  14–16" compo./cloth, 1949–1951 ....145.00–160.00
  14" cloth, vinyl head & limbs, 1950 only 135.00
  12" cloth/vinyl, 1965–1966 only 80.00
BUTCH, LITTLE 9" all vinyl, 1967–1968 only 125.00
BUTCH MCGUFFEY 22" compo./cloth, 1940–1941 ....200.00

18" BUNNY dolls, 1962.

Please read "About Pricing" for additional information.

C.U.   (see Collector's United under Special Events/Exclusives)
Cameo Lady   10", 1991 (see C.U. under Special Events/Exclusives)
Camelot   (see C.U. under Special Events/Exclusives)
Camille   21" compo., 1938–1939 (Wendy Ann) 2,200.00
Canada   8" hp., BK, #760, 1968–1972 (Wendy Ann) 125.00
    Straight leg, #0706, 1973–1975, marked "Alex." 60.00
    Straight legs, #560 (#534 in 1986), 1976–1988, (white face 1985–1987), marked "Alexander".....55.00
Candy Kid   11–15" compo., 1938–1941 (Wendy Ann) 275.00–375.00
Captain Hook   8" hp., #478, 1992–1993, Storyland Series (Peter Pan) (Wendy Ann).........................65.00
Carmen   (Dressed like Carmen Miranda, but not marked or meant as such.)
    7" compo., 1938–1943 (Tiny Betty) 285.00
    9–11" compo., 1938–1943, boy & girl (see also "Rumbero/Rumbera") (Little Betty) ...each 265.00–300.00
    11" compo., 1937–1939, has sleep eyes (Little Betty) 300.00
    14" compo., 1937–1940 (Wendy Ann) 365.00
    17" compo., 1939–1942 (Wendy Ann) 465.00

Plush Cats
With felt noses, glass eyes, and eyelashes.

21" compo., 1939–1942 (Wendy Ann) 750.00
21" compo., 1939–1942, Portrait with extra make-up, (Jacqueline) 1,400.00
14" plastic/vinyl, #1410, 1983–1986, Opera Series (Mary Ann) 85.00
10" hp., #1154, 1993, Portrette Series (Miranda), yellow/red 82.00
CARNVALE DOLL 1991 (see FAO Schwarz under Special Events/Exclusives)
CARNIVAL IN RIO 21" porcelain, 1989–1990 ....475.00
CARNIVAL IN VENICE 21" porcelain, 1990–1991 ....525.00
CAROLINE 15" vinyl, 1961–1962 only, in dresses, pants/jacket 300.00
In riding habit 400.00
As boy/boy hairstyle (nude) 95.00
In case/wardrobe ....1,400.00 up
CARREEN 14–17" compo., #1593, 1937–1938 (Wendy Ann) 800.00
14" plastic/vinyl, 1992–1993 (Louisa/Jennifer) 132.00
CARROT TOP 21" cloth, 1967 only 100.00
CASEY JONES 8" hp., 1991–1992 only, Americana Series 55.00
CASSOCK 8" hp., #511, 1989–1991 (Wendy Ann) 60.00
CATS 16, plush, dressed, glass eyes, long lashes, felt nose 365.00
CATHY 17–21" compo., 1939, 1946 (Wendy Ann) 750.00–900.00
CELIA'S DOLLS (see Special Events/Exclusives)
CENTURY OF FASHIONS 14" & 18" hp., 1954 (Margaret, Maggie & Cissy) 1,400.00–1,600.00
CHARITY 8" hp., #485, 1961 only, Americana Series, blue cotton dress (Wendy Ann) 2,200.00
CHARLENE 18" cloth/vinyl, 1991–1992 only 105.00
CHATTERBOX 24" plastic/vinyl talker, 1961 only ....285.00 up
CHEERLEADER 8", #324, 1990–1991 only, Americana Series (Wendy Ann) 55.00
8", 1990 (see I. Magnin under Special Events/Exclusives)
8" hp., #324, #324-1, 1992–1993, Americana Series, black or white doll, royal blue/gold outfit 52.00
CHERI 18" hp., 1954 only, Me & My Shadow Series, white satin gown, pink opera coat (Margaret) 1,400.00
CHERRY TWINS 8" hp., #388E, 1957 only (Wendy Ann) each ....each 1,200.00 up
CHERUB 12" vinyl, 1960–1961 ....75.00
18" hp. head/cloth & vinyl 80.00
26" 110.00
CHERUB BABIES Cloth, 1930's 475.00
CHILE 8" hp., #528, 1992 only (Wendy Ann) 55.00
CHILD AT HEART SHOP 8" Easter Bunny, 1990 (see Special Events/Exclusives)
CHINA 7" compo., 1936–1940 (Tiny Betty) 265.00
9" compo., 1935–1938 (Little Betty) 285.00
8" hp., BK, #772, 1972 (Wendy Ann) 125.00
8" (Maggie Mixup) 150.00
Straight leg, #0772–#572, 1973–1975, marked "Alex." 60.00
Straight legs, #572, 1976–1986, marked "Alexander" 55.00
#572, 1987–1989 (Maggie) 55.00
CHRISTENING BABY 11–13" cloth/vinyl, 1951–1954 ....80.00
16–19" 125.00
CHRISTMAS CANDY 14" #1544, 1993, Classic Series 115.00
CHRISTMAS SHOPPE (see Special Events/Exclusive)
CHRISTMAS CAROLING 10", #1149, 1992–1993, Portrette Series, burnt orange/gold dress 105.00
CHRISTMAS COOKIE 14", #1565, 1992 (Also see Lil Christmas Cookie, 8") (Louisa/Jennifer) 115.00
CHRISTMAS TREE TOPPER 1991 (see Spiegel's under Special Events/Exclusive)
CHURCHILL, LADY 18" hp., 1953 only, Beaux Arts Series (Margaret) ....1,400.00 up
CHURCHILL, SIR WINSTON 18" hp., 1953 only (Margaret) 1,250.00
CINDERELLA 7–8" compo., 1935–1944 (Tiny Betty) 285.00
9" compo., 1936–1941 (Little Betty) 300.00
13" compo., 1935–1937 (Wendy Ann) 365.00

14" compo., 1939 only, Sear's exclusive (Princess Elizabeth)..400.00
15" compo., 1935–1937 (Betty) 450.00
16–18" compo., 1935–1939 (Princess Elizabeth) 475.00–575.00
8" hp., #402, 1955 only (Wendy Ann)..700.00
8" hp., #498, 1990–1991, Storyland Series (Wendy Ann) 60.00
8", #476, 1992–1993, blue ballgown 66.00
8", #475, 1992 only, "Poor" outfit in blue w/black strips 52.00
12" hp., 1966 only, Literature Series (classic Lissy) 1,000.00
12" hp., 1966, "Poor" outfit 650.00
   1966, In window box with both outfits ....1,400.00 up
14" hp., 1950–1951, ballgown (Margaret)..750.00
14" hp., 1950–1951, "Poor" outfit (Margaret) 750.00
18" hp., 1950–1951 (Margaret)...825.00
14" plastic/vinyl, (#1440 to 1974; #1504 to 1991; #1541 in 1992) 1967–1992,
   "Poor" outfit (can be green, blue, gray or brown) (Mary Ann) 95.00
14", #140 on box, 1969 only, FAO Schwarz, all blue stain/gold trim, mint (Mary Ann) 325.00
14" plastic/vinyl, #1445, #1446, #1546, #1548, 1970–1983, Classic Series,
   dressed in pink (Mary Ann) 70.00
   #1548, #1549, 1984–1986, blue ballgown, two styles (Mary Ann)............................80.00
14" #1546, #1547, 1987–1991, Classic Series, white or blue ballgown (Mary Ann, Jennifer) 132.00
14" #1549, 1992 only, white/gold ballgown (Jennifer) 132.00
10", 1989, Disney World (see Special Events/Exclusives)
10", #1137, 1990–1991, Portrette Series, dressed in all pink (Cissette) 80.00

14" CINDERELLA, 1970–1983

10" CISSETTE in formal/ballgown.

20" CISSY, mid-1950's.

CISSETTE 10–11" hp., 1957–1963, must have good face color, in various street dresses .... 225.00 up
   In formals, ballgowns .... 600.00 up
   Coats & hat 300.00
   1961 only, beauty queen with trophy 200.00
   Special gift set/three wigs .... 1,200.00 up
      Doll only, clean with good face color 135.00
   1954, Queen/trunk/trousseau 900.00
CISSY 20" hp. (also 21"), 1955–1959, must have good face color, in various street dresses .... 300.00 up
   In ballgowns .... 650.00 up
   Trunk/wardrobe .... 1,500.00 up
   1950's magazine ads using doll 10.00
CISSY GODEY 21" porcelain, 1993, bride 570.00
CIVIL WAR 18" hp., #2010B, 1953 only, Glamour Girls Series (Margaret) 1,300.00
   8" hp., #0201, 1953–1954 (Wendy Ann) 1,200.00
CLARA & THE NUTCRACKER 14", #1564, 1992 only (Louisa/Jennifer) 92.00
CLARABELLE CLOWN 19", 1951–1953 .... 350.00
   29" 500.00
   49" 750.00
CLAUDETTE 10", #1123 (in peach), 1988–1989, Portrette Series (Cissette) 80.00
CLEOPATRA 12", #1315, 1980–1985, Portraits of History Series 52.00

CLEVELAND, FRANCES   1985–1987, 4th set First Ladies/Presidents' Ladies Series (Mary Ann) 80.00
CLOVER KID   7" compo., 1935–1936 (Tiny Betty) 275.00
CLOWN   8", #305, 1990–1992 only, Americana Series, has painted face (Maggie)........................58.00
    BOBO   8" hp., #310, 1991–1992 (Wendy Ann) 55.00
    STILTS   8" #320, 1992–1993, doll on stilts..60.00
    PIERROT   8", #561, 1956 only (Wendy Ann) 1,200.00
COCO   21" plastic/vinyl, 1966, in various clothes (other than Portrait) ....2,000.00 up
    10", #1140, 1989–1992, Portrette Series, dressed in all black (Cissette) 78.00
COLUMBUS, CHRISTOPHER   8" hp., #328, 1992 only, Americana Series....................................80.00
COLLECTOR UNITED DOLLS   (see Special Events/Exclusives)
COLLEEN   10", #1121, 1988 only, Portrette Series, in green (Cissette)....................................85.00
COLONIAL   7" compo., 1937–1938 (Tiny Betty) 265.00
    9" compo., 1936–1939 (Little Betty) 285.00
    8" hp., BKW, #389, #789, 1962–1964 (Wendy Ann) 375.00
CONFEDERATE OFFICER   12", 1990–1991, Scarlett Series (Wendy Ann)...............................80.00
    8" hp., 1991–1992, Scarlett Series (see Ashley)
COOKIE   19" compo./cloth, 1938–1940 ....450.00
COOLIDGE, GRACE   14", 1989–1990, 6th set Presidents' Ladies/First Ladies Series (Louisa) 100.00
CORNELIA   21", #2191, 1972, Portrait Series, dressed in pink with full cape (Jacqueline) 600.00
    #2191, 1973, pink with ¾–length jacket 550.00
    #2296, 1974, blue with black trim 475.00

21" CORNELIA, 1975

#2290, 1975, rose red with black trim and hat 450.00

#2293, 1976, pink with black trim and hat 375.00

#2212, 1978, blue with full cape 325.00

Cloth/felt, 1930's 750.00

COUNTRY CHRISTMAS 14", #1543, 1991–1992 only, Classic Series (Mary Ann) 132.00

COUNTRY COUSINS 10" cloth, 1940's 350.00

26" cloth, 1940's 485.00

30" cloth, 1940's 675.00

16½", 1958, mint (Marybel) 375.00

COURTNEY AND FRIENDS (see Alexander Doll Co. under Special Events/Exclusives)

COUSIN GRACE 8" hp., BKW, #432, 1957 only (Wendy Ann) ....2,200.00 up

COUSIN KAREN 8" hp., BKW, #620, 1956 only (Wendy Ann) 1,800.00

COUSIN MARIE & MARY 8" hp., (Marie - #465; Mary - #462) 1963 only (Wendy Ann) ....each 1,400.00

COWARDLY LION 8", #431, 1993, Storybook Series 62.00

COWBOY 8" hp., BK, #732, 1967–1969, Americana Series (Wendy Ann) 385.00

8", 1987 (see M.A.D.C. under Special Events/Exclusives)

COWGIRL 8" hp., BK, #724, 1967–1970, Americana/Storybook Series (Wendy Ann) 365.00

10", #1132, 1990–1991, Portrette Series, white/red outfit (Cissette) 82.00

CRETE 8" straight leg, #529, 1987 only (white face) 58.00

CROCKETT, DAVY BOY OR GIRL 8" hp., 1955 only, (Boy - #446; Girl - #443) (Wendy Ann) ....650.00 up

CRY DOLLY 14–16" vinyl, 1953, 12-piece layette 175.00

14", 16", 19" in swimsuit 100.00–135.00

16–19" all vinyl, dress or rompers 125.00–150.00

CUDDLY 10½" cloth, 1942–1944 ....365.00

17" cloth, 1942–1944 ....400.00

CURLY LOCKS 8" hp., #472, 1955 only (Wendy Ann) 900.00

8" straight leg, #421, 1987–1988, Storybook Series 70.00

CYNTHIA 15" hp., 1952 only (black "Margaret") 1,000.00

18", 1952 only 1,200.00

23", 1952 only 1,500.00

CZECHOSLOVAKIA 8" hp., BK, #764, 1972 (Wendy Ann) 135.00

Straight leg, #0764, #564, 1973–1975, marked "Alex." 60.00

Straight leg, #536, 1976–1987, marked "Alexander" 55.00

8", #536, 1985–1987, white face 55.00

8", #521, reintroduced 1992–1993 (Wendy Ann) 57.00

7" compo., 1935–1937 (Tiny Betty) 245.00

Please read "About Pricing" for additional information.

DAFFY DOWN DILLEY 8" straight legs, #429, 1986 only, Storybook Series (Wendy Ann) 80.00

    8", #429, Storybook Series, 1987–1988 (Maggie) 60.00

DAHL, ARLENE 18" hp., 1950–1951 (Maggie) ....2,800.00 up

DAISY 10", #1110, 1987–1989, Portrette Series, yellow with overlace (Cissette) 85.00

DANISH 7" compo., 1937–1941 (Tiny Betty) 265.00

    9" compo., 1938–1940 (Little Betty) 285.00

DARE, VIRGINIA 9" compo., 1940–1941 (Little Betty) 300.00

DARLENE 18" cloth/vinyl, 1991–1992 ....105.00

DAVID & DIANE 8", 1989 (see FAO Schwarz under Special Events/Exclusives)

DAVID COPPERFIELD 7" compo., 1936–1938 (Tiny Betty) 300.00

    14" compo., 1938 only (Wendy Ann) 650.00

    16" cloth, early 1930's, Dicken's character ....675.00 up

DAVID, LITTLE RABBI 1991 (see Celia's Dolls under Special Events/Exclusives)

DAVID QUACK-A-FIELD OR TWISTAIL Cloth/felt, 1930's 675.00

DAY OF WEEK DOLLS 7", 1935–1940 (Tiny Betty) ....each 400.00

    9–11" compo., 1936–1938 (Little Betty) ....each 300.00

    13" compo., 1939 (Wendy Ann) 450.00

10" DAISY
Portrette Series, 1987–1989

DECEMBER 14", #1528, 1989 only, Classic Series (Mary Ann) 95.00
DEAREST 12" vinyl baby, 1962–1964 ....100.00
DEBRA (DEBORAH) 21", 1949–1951, Portrette, ballerina with extra make-up (Margaret)..............2,600.00 up
    21", 1949–1951, bride with five-piece layered bustle in back..2,600.00 up
DEBUTANTE 18" hp., 1953 only (Maggie)...950.00 up
DEFOE, DR. 14" compo., 1937–1939 ....1,500.00 up
    15–16" compo., 1937–1939 ....1,500.00
DEGAS 21" compo., 1945–1946, Portrait (Wendy Ann) ....2,200.00 up
DEGAS GIRL 14", #1475 (#1575 from 1974), 1967–1987,
Portrait Children & Fine Art Series (Mary Ann) 70.00
DENMARK 10" hp., 1962–1963 (Cissette) 980.00
    8" hp., BK, #769, 1970–1972 (Wendy Ann) 125.00
    8" hp., straight leg, #0769-569, 1973–1975, marked "Alex." (Wendy Ann).......................60.00
    8" hp., straight leg, #546, 1976–1989, marked "Alexander" (1985-1987 white face) (Wendy Ann) 55.00
    8" reintroduced, #519, 1991 only (Wendy Ann) 55.00
DESERT STORM (see "Welcome Home")
DIANA 14", 1993, Anne/Green Gables Series, trunk and wardrobe...260.00
DIAMOND LIL (see M.A.D.C. under Special Events/Exclusives)
DICKINSON, EMILY 14", #1587, 1989 only, Classic Series (Mary Ann)......................................90.00
DICKSIE & DUCKSIE Cloth/felt, 1930's ....500.00 up
DILLY DALLY SALLY 7" compo., 1937–1942 (Tiny Betty) 265.00
    9" compo., 1938–1939 (Little Betty) 285.00
DING DONG BELL 7" compo., 1937–1942 (Tiny Betty) 265.00
DINNER AT EIGHT 10", #1127, 1989–1991, Portrette Series, black/white dress (Cissette).....................62.00
DINOSAUR 8" hp., #343, 1993, Americana Series 55.00
DIONNE QUINTS Original mint or very slight craze.
    20" compo. toddlers, 1938–1939 ....750.00 each   4,300.00 set
    19" compo. toddlers, 1936–1938 ....700.00 each   4,200.00 set
    16–17" compo. toddlers, 1937–1939 ....650.00 each   3,600.00 set
    14" compo. toddlers, 1937–1938 ....450.00 each   2,450.00 set
    11" compo. toddlers, 1937–1938, wigs & sleep eyes ....300.00 each   2,000.00 set
    11" compo. toddlers, 1937–1938, molded hair & sleep eyes ...300.00 each   2,000.00 set
    11" compo. babies, 1936, wigs & sleep eyes ....300.00 each   2,000.00 set
    11" compo. babies, 1936, molded hair & sleep eyes ....300.00 each   2,000.00 set

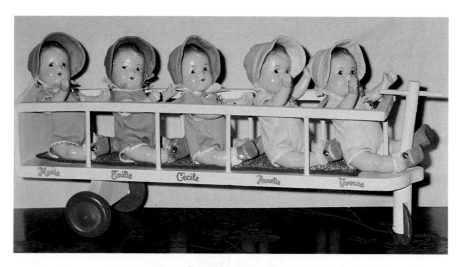

Set of 8" DIONNE QUINTS.
Priced more than book due to scooter.

8" compo. toddlers, 1935–1939, molded hair & painted eyes ....160.00 each   1,200.00 set
8" compo. toddlers, 1935–1939, wigs and painted eyes ....160.00 each   1,200.00 set
14" cloth body/compo., 1938 ....550.00 each   3,200.00 set
17" cloth body/compo., 1938 ....600.00 each   3,500.00 set
22" cloth/compo., 1936–1937 ....675.00
24" all cloth, 1935–1936..1,100.00
16" all cloth, 1935–1936 ....800.00 up

DISNEY (see Special Events/Exclusives)
DOLL FINDERS (see Special Events/Exclusives)
DOLLS OF THE MONTH 7–8" compo., 1937–1939, Birthday Dolls (Tiny Betty) 275.00
DOLLS 'N BEARLAND (see Special Events/Exclusives)
DOLLY 8", #436, 1988–1989, Storybook Series (Wendy Ann)..80.00
DOLLY DEARS (see Special Events/Exclusives)
DOLLY DRYPER 11" vinyl, 1952 only, 7-piece layette 80.00
DOMINICAN REPUBLIC 8" straight leg, #544, 1986–1988 (1985–1986 white face)...................60.00
DOROTHY 14", #1532, 1990–1993, all blue/white check dress and solid blue pinafore (Mary Ann) ..85.00
    8" hp., #464, 1991–1993, blue/white check, white bodice (Wendy Ann) 52.00
DOTTIE DUMBUNNIE Cloth/felt, 1930's ....700.00 up
DRESSED FOR OPERA 18" hp., 1953 only (Margaret) ....1,400.00 up
DRUCILLA (see M.A.D.C. under Special Events/Exclusives)
DUDE RANCH 8" hp., #449, 1955 only (Wendy Ann) ....675.00 up
DUMPLIN' BABY 20–23½", 1957–1958 ....200.00
DUTCH 7" compo., 1935–1939 (Tiny Betty) 245.00
    9" compo boy or girl, 1936–1941 ....275.00
    8" hp., BKW, #777, 1964, boy* (Wendy Ann)..150.00
    BK, #777, #0777, 1965–1972 ....125.00
    8" hp., straight leg, #777, *0777, 1972–1973, marked "Alex." 60.00
    8" hp., BKW, #391-791, 1961–1964, girl* 150.00
    8" hp. BK, #791, 1965–1972 ....60.00
    8" BKW, #791, 1964 only (Maggie Mixup)..175.00
DUTCH LULLABY 8", #499, 1993, Wynkin, Blynkin, & Nod, in wooden shoe, as set only.................205.00

* Both became NETHERLAND *in 1974.*

E

Please read "About Pricing" for additional information.

Easter Doll 8" hp., 1968 only, special for West Coast, in yellow dress (Wendy Ann) ....1,200.00 up
   7½", SLNW, #361, 1953, organdy dress, doll carries basket with chicken ....600.00 up
   14" plastic/vinyl, 1968 only (Mary Ann) ....800.00 up
Easter Bonnet 14", #1562, 1992 (Louisa/Jennifer) 145.00
Easter Bunny 8", 1990 (see Child at Heart under Special Events/Exclusives)
Easter Sunday 8" hp., #340 or #340-1, 1993, Americana Series, black or white doll 65.00
Ecuador 8" hp., BK & BKW, #878, 1963–1966 (Wendy Ann) 365.00
Edith, The Lonely Doll 16" plastic/vinyl, 1958–1959 ....375.00
   22", 1958–1959 ....450.00
   8" hp., #850, 1958 only (Wendy Ann) 625.00
Edith with Golden Hair 18" cloth, 1940's 625.00
Edwardian 18" hp., 1953 only, Glamour Girl Series (Margaret) 1,600.00
   8" hp., #0200, 1953 only (Wendy Ann) 1,200.00
Eisenhower, Mamie 14", 1989–1990, 6th set Presidents' Ladies/First Ladies Series (Mary Ann).......100.00
Egypt 8" straight leg, #543, 1986–1989 (Wendy Ann) 86.00
Egyptian 7–8" compo., 1936–1940 (Tiny Betty) 265.00
   9" compo., 1936–1940 (Little Betty) 285.00
Elaine 18" hp., 1954 only, Me & My Shadow Series, blue organdy dress (Cissy) 1,450.00
   8" hp., #0035E, 1954 only, matches 18" (Wendy Ann) 1,300.00
Elise 16½" hp./vinyl arms (18", 1963 only), 1957–1964, jointed ankles & knees, good face color
   In street clothes ....220.00 up
   In ballgown, formal, or Portrait ....400.00 up
   With Marybel face 400.00

14" Easter Bonnet, 1992

17" Elise using the "Marybel" head.

In riding habit, 1963 (Marybel face)..450.00
Ballerina 200.00
With Marybel head, 1962 only..275.00
18", 1963 only, with bouffant hairstyle 300.00
17" hp./vinyl, 1961–1962, one-piece arms & legs, jointed ankles & knees,....................325.00
18" hp./vinyl, 1963–1964, jointed ankles & knees 350.00
    In riding habit 400.00
17" plastic/vinyl, 1966 only, street dress...225.00
17", 1966–1972, in trunk/trousseau ....850.00 up
17" Portrait, 1972–1973 ....250.00
17", 1966, 1976–1977, in formal 250.00
17", 1966–1987, Bride 145.00
17", 1966–1991, Ballerina 125.00–175.00
17", 1966–1989, in any discontinued costume ....145.00 up
ELISE LESLIE 14", #1560, 1988 only (Mary Ann) 95.00
ELIZA 14", #1544, 1991 only, Classic Series (Louisa) 155.00
EMILY Cloth/felt, 1930's...625.00
EMPRESS ELIZABETH 1991 (see My Doll House under Special Events/Exclusives)
ENCHANTED DOLL (see Special Events/Exclusives)
ENCHANTED EVENING 21" Portrait, 1991–1992 only, different necklace than shown in catalog (Cissy)....280.00
ENGLISH GUARD 8" hp., BK, #764, 1966–1968, Portrait Children Series (Wendy Ann) 325.00
    8", #515, reintroduced 1989–1991, marked "Alexander" (Wendy Ann) 55.00
ESKIMO 8" hp., BK, #723, 1967–1969, Americana Series (Wendy Ann)..............................325.00
    9" compo., 1936–1939 (Little Betty) 250.00
    With Maggie Mixup face 325.00
ESTONIA 8" straight leg, #545, 1986–1987 only (Wendy Ann)....................................75.00
EVA LOVELACE 7" compo., 1935 only (Tiny Betty) 265.00
    Cloth, 1935 only...625.00
EVANGELINE 18" cloth, 1930's 600.00

21" ENCHANTED EVENING, 1991

Please read "About Pricing" for additional information.

F.A.O. Schwarz (see Special Events/Exclusives)
Fairy Godmother 14", #1550, #1551, #1568, 1983–1992, Classic Series (Mary Ann, Louisa) ...85.00–165.00
   Fairy outfit, 1983, M.A.D.C. (see Special Events/Exclusives)
   10" Portrette, #1156, 1993, blue/gold gown (Cissette) 95.00
Fairy Princess 7–8" compo., 1940–1943 (Tiny Betty) 285.00
   9" compo., 1939–1941 (Little Betty) 300.00
   11" compo., 1939 only (Wendy Ann)..375.00
   15–18" compo., 1939–1942 (Wendy Ann) 650.00–750.00
   21–22" compo., 1939, 1944–1946 (Wendy Ann) 950.00
Fairy Queen 14½" compo., 1940–1946 (Wendy Ann)...650.00
   18" compo., 1940–1946 (Wendy Ann)..750.00
   18" hp., 1949–1950 (Margaret) 900.00
   14½" hp., 1948–1950 (Margaret) 725.00
Fairy Tales – Dumas 9" compo., 1937–1941 (Little Betty) 300.00
Faith 8" hp., #486, 1961 only, Americana Group, plaid jumper/organdy blouse (Wendy Ann)...2,200.00 up
   8" hp. (see C.U. under Special Events/Exclusives)
Fantasy 8", 1990 (see Doll Finders under Special Events/Exclusives)
Fannie Elizabeth 8" (see Belks under Special Events/Exclusives)
Farmer's Daughter 8", 1991 (see Enchanted Doll House under Special Events/Exclusives)

14" Fairy Godmother, 1992

FASHIONS OF THE CENTURY 14–18" hp., 1954–1955 (Margaret, Maggie) 1,600.00
FILLMORE, ABIGAIL 1982–1984, 3rd set Presidents' Ladies/First Ladies Series (Louisa) 90.00
FINDLAY, JANE 1979–1981, 1st set Presidents' Ladies/First Ladies Series (Mary Ann) 110.00
FINLAND 8" hp., BK, #767, 1968–1972 (Wendy Ann) 125.00
    8" hp., straight leg, #0767-567, 1973–1975, marked "Alex." 55.00
    8" hp., straight leg, #567, 1976–1987, marked "Alexander" (1985–1987 white face) 50.00
FINNISH 7" compo., 1935–1937 (Tiny Betty) 235.00
FIRST COMES LOVE BRIDE 1993 (see C.U. under Special Events/Exclusives)
FIRST COMMUNION 8" hp., #395, 1957 only (Wendy Ann) ....750.00 up
    14", #1545, 1991–1992 only, Classics Series (Louisa) 95.00
FIRST LADIES (see "Presidents' Ladies")
FIRST MODERN DOLL CLUB (see Special Events/Exclusives)
FISHER QUINTS 7" hp./vinyl, 1964 only (Little Genius) 500.00
FIVE LITTLE PEPPERS 13" & 16" compo, 1936 only ....each 500.00–600.00
FLAPPER 10", Portrette Series, 1988–1991 (Cissette) 70.00
    10", #1118, 1988, red dress (all white dress in 1991) (see under M.A.D.C. in Special Events/Exclusives)
FLORA MCFLIMSEY (with and without "e").
    9" compo., 1938–1941 (Little Betty) 325.00
    22" compo., 1938–1944 (Princess Elizabeth) ....800.00 up
    15–16" compo., 1938–1944 (Princess Elizabeth) ....550.00 up
    16–17" compo., 1936–1937 (Wendy Ann) ....550.00 up
    14" compo., 1938–1944 (Princess Elizabeth) ....500.00 up
    12" compo., 1944 only, holds 5" "Nancy Ann" doll, tagged "Margie Ann" (Wendy Ann) ...600.00 up
    15" Miss Flora McFlimsey, vinyl head, 1953 only (Cissy) 600.00
FLOWERGIRL 16"–18" compo., 1939, 1944–1947 (Princess Elizabeth) 500.00
    20–24" compo., 1939, 1944–1947 (Princess Elizabeth) 650.00
    15–18" hp., 1954 only (Cissy) 425.00–525.00
    15" hp., 1954 only (Margaret) 600.00
    8" hp., #602, 1956 (Wendy Ann) 650.00
    8" hp., #334, 1992–1993, Americana Series, white doll (Wendy Ann) 55.00
    8", #334-1, 1992 only, black doll 55.00
    10", #1122, 1988–1990, Portrette Series, pink dotted Swiss dress (Cissette) 85.00
FRANCE 7" compo., 1936–1943 (Tiny Betty) 235.00
    9" compo., 1937–1941 (Little Betty) 250.00
    8" hp., BKW, #390, #790, 1961–1965 (Wendy Ann) 175.00
    8" hp., BK, #790, 1965–1972 ....125.00
    8" hp., straight leg, #0790, #590, 1973–1975, marked "Alex." 60.00
    8" straight leg, #590, #552, #517, #582, 1976–1992, marked "Alexander" (1985–1987 white face)...55.00
    1985–1987, #590, #552, white face 50.00
FRENCH ARISTOCRAT 10" Portrette, #1143, 1991–1992 only, bright pink/white (Cissette) 112.00
FRENCH FLOWERGIRL 8" hp., #610, 1956 only (Wendy Ann) ....650.00 up
FRIAR TUCK 8" hp., #493, 1989–1991, Storybook Series (Maggie Mixup) 65.00
FRIEDRICH (see "Sound of Music")
FROU-FROU 40" all cloth, 1951 only, ballerina with yarn hair dressed in green or lilac ....700.00 up
FUNNY 18" cloth, 1963–1977 ....55.00

Please read "About Pricing" for additional information.

GAINSBOROUGH 20" hp., 1957, Models Formals Series, taffeta gown, large picture hat (Cissy)......1,000.00 up
 #2184, 21" hp./vinyl arms, 1968, blue with white lace jacket (Jacqueline) 650.00
 #2192, 21", 1972, yellow with full white overlace (Jacqueline) 600.00
 #2192, 21", 1973, pale blue, scallop lace overskirt (Jacqueline)...500.00
 #2211, 21", 1978, pink with full lace overdress (Jacqueline) 450.00
   10" (Cissette) 450.00
GARDEN PARTY 18" hp., 1953 only (Margaret) 1,600.00
 20" hp., 1956–1957 (Cissy) ....900.00 up
 8" hp., #488, 1955 only (Wendy Ann)...1,200.00
GARFIELD, LUCRETIA 1985–1987, 4th set Presidents' Ladies/First Ladies Series (Louisa).....................80.00
GENIUS BABY 21"–30" plastic/vinyl, 1960–1961, has flirty eyes 125.00–165.00
 Little, 8" hp. head/vinyl, 1956–1962 (see Little Genius)
GEPETTO 8", #478, 1993, Storybook Series 50.00
GERANIUM 9" early vinyl toddler, 1953 only, red organdy dress & bonnet 100.00
GERMAN (GERMANY) 8" hp., BK, #763, 1966–1972 (Wendy Ann) 125.00
 8" hp., straight leg, #0763-563, 1973–1975, marked "Alex." 60.00
 10" hp., 1962–1963 (Cissette)..1,250.00
 8" straight legs, #563, #535, #506, 1976–1989, marked "Alexander" (1985–1987 white face) 58.00
 8", 1990–1991, marked "Alexander" 60.00
 8", #535, 1986, white face 50.00

21" GODEY, 1977

GIBSON GIRL   10" hp., 1962, eye shadow (Cissette) 800.00
   1963, plain blouse with no stripes 700.00
   16" cloth, 1930's 775.00
   10", #1124, 1988–1990, Portrette Series, red and black (Cissette) 80.00
GIDGET   14" plastic/vinyl, #1415, #1420, #1421, 1966 only (Mary Ann) 350.00
GIGI   14", #1597, 1986–1987, Classic Series (Mary Ann) 70.00
GIRL ON FLYING TRAPEZE   40" cloth, 1951 only, dressed in pink satin tutu 750.00
GLAMOUR GIRLS   18" hp., 1953 only (Margaret, Maggie) 1,600.00
GLENDA, THE GOOD WITCH   8", #473, 1992–1993, Storyland Series (Wendy Ann) 62.00
GODEY   21" compo., 1945–1947 (Wendy Ann) 1,600.00
   14" hp., 1950–1951 (Margaret) 1,200.00
   20" hp., 1951 only (Margaret) 1,500.00
   18" hp., 1953 only, Glamour Girl Series (Maggie) 1,400.00
   21" hp., vinyl straight arms, 1961 only (Cissy) 1,200.00
   21", #2153, 1965, dressed in all red, blonde hair (Jacqueline) 675.00
   21" hp., vinyl arms, #2172, 1967, dressed in pink & ecru (Jacqueline) 600.00
     #2195, 1969, red with black trim 500.00
     #2195, 1970, pink with burgundy short jacket 400.00
     #2161, 1971, pink, black trim, short jacket 375.00
     #2298, 1977, ecru with red jacket and bonnet 350.00
   8" SLW, #491, 1955 only (Wendy Ann) ....1,200.00 up
   10" hp., #1172, 1968, dressed in all pink with bows down front (Cissette) 450.00
     #1172, 1969, all yellow with bows down front 500.00
     #1183, 1970, all lace pink dress with natural straw hat 650.00
   21" plastic/vinyl, 1966 only, red with black short jacket & hat (Coco) 2,300.00
GODEY BRIDE   14" hp., 1950 (Margaret) ....825.00 up
   18" hp., 1950–1951 (Margaret) 975.00
   21" porcelain, 1993 (Cissy) 570.00
GODEY GROOM/MAN   14" hp., 1950 (Margaret) 1,050.00
   18" hp., 1950–1951 (Margaret) 1,200.00
GODEY LADY   14" hp., 1950 (Margaret) 1,100.00
   18" hp., 1950–1951 (Margaret) 1,200.00
GOLDFISH   8" hp., #344, Americana Series 72.00
GOLD RUSH   10" hp., 1963 only (Cissette) 1,400.00
GOLDILOCKS   18" cloth, 1930's ....600.00 up
   7–8" compo., 1938–1942 (Tiny Betty) 275.00
   18" hp., 1951 only (Maggie) ....1,000.00 up
   14" plastic/vinyl, #1520, 1978–1979, Classic Series, satin dress (Mary Ann) 80.00
   14", #1520, 1980–1983, blue satin or cotton dress (Mary Ann) 70.00
   14", #1553, 1991 only, Classic Series, long side curls tied with ribbon (Mary Ann) 95.00
   8", #497, 1990–1991 only, Storyland Series (1991 dress in different plaid) (Wendy Ann) 60.00
GONE WITH THE WIND (SCARLETT)   14", #1490, #1590, 1969–1986,
   all white dress/green sash (Mary Ann) 85.00
GOOD FAIRY   14" hp., 1969 (Margaret) ....700.00 up
GOOD LITTLE GIRL   16" cloth, 1966 only, mate to "Bad Little Girl," wears pink dress 125.00
GOYA   8" hp., #314, 1953 only (Wendy Ann) ....1,000.00 up
   21" hp./vinyl arms, #2183, 1968, multi-tiered pink dress (Jacqueline) 700.00
   21", #2235, 1982–1983, maroon dress with black Spanish lace (Jacqueline) 300.00
GRADUATION   8" hp., #399, 1957 only (Wendy Ann) ....1,000.00 up
   12", 1957 only (Lissy) 900.00
   8", #307, 1990–1991, Americana Series (white doll only) (Wendy Ann) 55.00
   8", #307, #307-1, 1991–1992, Americana Series, white or black doll 55.00
GRANDMA JANE   14" plastic/vinyl, #1420, 1970–1972 (Mary Ann) 285.00

GRANT, JULIA   1982–1984, 3rd set First Ladies/Presidents' Ladies Series (Louisa) 90.00
GRAVE, ALICE   18" cloth, 1930's ....600.00 up
GRAYSON, KATHRYN   20–21" hp., 1949 only (Margaret) ....2,400.00 up
GREAT BRITAIN   8" hp., #558, 1977–1988 (1985–1987 white face) (Wendy Ann) 55.00
GREECE BOY   8" hp., #527, 1992–1993 (Wendy Ann) 52.00
GREEK BOY   8" hp., BK & BKW, #769, 1965–1968 (Wendy Ann) 345.00
GREEK GIRL   8" hp., BK, #765, 1968–1972 (Wendy Ann)...125.00
    8" hp., straight leg, #0765, #565, 1973–1975, marked "Alex." 60.00
    8" hp., straight leg, #565, #527, 1976–1987 (1985–1987 white face), marked "Alexander" 55.00
GRETEL   7" compo., 1935–1942 (Tiny Betty) 245.00
    9" compo., 1938–1940 (Little Betty) 285.00
    18" hp., 1948 only (Margaret) ....1,000.00 up
    7½–8" hp., SLW, #470, 1955 (Wendy Ann) ....600.00 up
    8" hp., BK, #754, 1966–1972, Storybook Series (Wendy Ann) 125.00
    8" hp., straight leg, #0754, #454, 1973–1975, marked "Alex." 60.00
    8" hp., straight leg, #454, 1976–1986 (1986 white face), marked "Alexander" 52.00
    8" hp., #462, 1991–1992 only, Storyland Series, reintroduced doll (Wendy Ann) 52.00
GRETEL BRINKER   12", 1993 (Lissy) 95.00
GRETL   (see "Sound of Music")
GROOM   18" – 21" compo., 1946–1947, mint (Margaret) 1,000.00
    18–21" hp., 1949–1951 (Margaret) ....850.00 up
    14–16" hp., 1949–1951 (Margaret) ....600.00 up
    7½" hp., SL & SLW, #577, #464, #466, 1953–1955 (Wendy Ann) ....425.00 up
    8" BK, #577, 1956 ....425.00
    8" BK, #377, 1957 ....425.00
    8" BK, #572, 1958 ....425.00
    8" hp., BK, #421, #442, 1961–1963 (Wendy Ann) ....350.00 up
    8", #488, #388, reintroduced 1989–1991 only (Wendy Ann) 65.00
    8", #339, 1993, black pants, peach tie, white jacket..55.00
GUENIVERE   10", #1146, 1992 only, Portrette Series, forest green/gold 95.00

Please read "About Pricing" for additional information.

HALLOWEEN WITCH 8" C.U. (see Special Events/Exclusives)
HAMLET 12", Romance Collection (Nancy Drew) 90.00
    12", 1993 (Lissy) 95.00
HANS BRINKER 12", 1993 (Lissy) 95.00
HANSEL 7" compo., 1935–1942 (Tiny Betty) 275.00
    9" compo., 1938–1940 (Little Betty) 300.00
    18" hp., 1948 only (Margaret) ....1,000.00 up
    8" hp., SLW, #470, 1955 only (Wendy Ann) ....600.00 up
    8" hp., BK, #753, 1966–1972, Storybook Series (Wendy Ann) 125.00
    8" hp., straight leg, #0753, #543, 1973–1975, marked "Alex." 60.00
    8" hp., straight leg, #543, 1976–1986 (1986 white face), marked "Alexander" 52.00
    8" hp., #461, 1991–1992 only, Storyland Series, reintroduced doll (Wendy Ann) 50.00
HAPPY 20" cloth/vinyl, 1970 only 260.00
HAPPY BIRTHDAY M.A.D.C., 1985 (see Special Events/Exclusives)
    8" hp., #325, #325-1, 1992–1993, Americana Series, black or white doll (Wendy Ann) 60.00
HAPPY BIRTHDAY BILLIE 8" hp., #345, #345-1, Americana Series, black or white boy 60.00
HARDING, FLORENCE 1988, 5th set Presidents' Ladies/First Ladies Series (Louisa) 70.00
HARRISON, CAROLINE 1985–1987, 4th set Presidents' Ladies/First Ladies Series (Louisa) 80.00
HAWAII 8", #301, 1990–1991 only, Americana Series, (Wendy Ann) 60.00
HAWAIIAN 8" hp., BK, #722, 1966–1969, Americana Series (Wendy Ann) ....435.00 up
    7" compo., 1936–1939 (Tiny Betty) 265.00
    9" compo., 1937–1944 (Little Betty) 300.00
HAYES, LUCY 1985–1987, 4th set Presidents' Ladies/First Ladies Series (Louisa) 80.00
HEATHER 18" cloth/vinyl, 1990 only 95.00
HEIDI 7" compo., 1938–1939 (Tiny Betty) 265.00
    14" plastic/vinyl, #1480, #1580, #1581, 1969–1985, Classic Series (Mary Ann) 65.00
    14", #1581, 1986–1988, solid green dress, floral apron 75.00
    8" hp., #460, 1991–1992, Storyland Series (Maggie) 55.00
HELLO BABY 22", 1962 only 125.00
HENIE, SONJA 13–15" compo., 1939–1942 ....600.00
    7" compo., 1939–1942 (Tiny Betty) 325.00
    9" compo., 1940–1941 (Little Betty) 400.00
    11" compo. (Wendy Ann) 525.00
    14" compo. 600.00
    14" in case/wardrobe ....1,000.00 up
    17–18" compo. 950.00
    20–23" compo. 1,100.00
    13–14" compo., jointed waist 675.00
    15–18" hp./vinyl, 1951 only, no extra joints, must have good face color (Madeline) 850.00
HER LADY AND CHILD (THUMBELINA) 21" porcelain, 8" hp., #010, 1992–1993, limited to 2,500 ....510.00
HIAWATHA 8" hp., #720, 1967–1969, Americana Series (Wendy Ann) 375.00
    7" compo. (Tiny Betty) 285.00
    18" cloth, early 1930's 650.00
HIGHLAND FLING 8" hp., #484, 1955 only (Wendy Ann) 575.00
HILDA 18" compo., black doll, 1947 only (Margaret) ....1,200.00 up
HOLIDAY ON ICE 8" hp., #319, 1992–1993, red with white fur hat and muff (Wendy Ann) 55.00
HOLLAND 7" compo., 1936–1943 (Tiny Betty) 225.00
HOLLY 10", #1135, 1990–1991, Portrette Series, white/red roses (Cissette) 90.00
HONEYBEA 12" vinyl, 1963 only 135.00
HONEYETTE BABY 16" compo./cloth, 1941–1942 ....125.00
    7" compo., 1934–1937, little girl dress (Tiny Betty) 200.00

HONEYBUN 18–19", 1951–1952 only 120.00
    23–26" 145.00
HONEYMOON IN NEW ORLEANS 8" (see Scarlett)
HOOVER, LOU 14", 1989–1990, 6th set First Ladies/Presidents' Ladies Series (Mary Ann) 100.00
HUCKLEBERRY FINN 8" hp., #490, 1989–1991 only, Storybook Series (Wendy Ann) 58.00
HULDA 18" hp., 1949 only (Margaret) ....1,500.00 up
    14" hp., 1948–1949 ....950.00 up
HUGGUMS, LITTLE 14", 1986 only, molded hair...45.00
    12", 1963–1993, molded hair, available in seven outfits...42.00 up
    12", 1963–1982, 1988, rooted hair ....42.00 up
    1991, special outfits for Imaginarium Shop (see Special Events/Exclusives)
HUGGUMS, LIVELY 25", 1963 only, knob makes limbs and head move 125.00
HUGGUMS, BIG 25", 1963–1979, boy or girl...85.00
HUNGARIAN (HUNGARY) 8" hp., BKW, #397, #797, 1962–1965 (Wendy Ann) 175.00
    BK, #397, with metal crown..185.00
    BK, #797, 1965–1972 ....145.00
    8" hp., straight leg, #0797, #597, 1973–1976, marked "Alex." 60.00
    8" hp., straight leg, #597, 1976–1986 (1986 white face), marked "Alexander" 55.00
    8" hp., #522, reintroduced 1992 (Wendy Ann) 50.00
HYACINTH 9" early vinyl toddler, 1953 only, blue dress & bonnet 100.00

14" hard plastic HULDA, 1948

Please read "About Pricing" for additional information.

IBIZA 8", #510, 1989 only (Wendy Ann) 80.00
ICE CAPADES 1950's (Cissy)...1,200.00 up
    1960's (Jacqueline)..1,500.00 up
ICE SKATER 8" hp., BK & BKW, #555, 1955–1956 (Wendy Ann) ....550.00 up
    8", #303, 1990–1991 only, Americana Series, purple/silver (Wendy Ann) 60.00
ICELAND 10", 1962–1963 (Cissette)...1,200.00
IMAGINARIUM SHOP (see Special Events/Exclusives)
I. MAGNIN STORE (see Special Events/Exclusives)
INDIA 8" hp., BKW, #775, 1965 (Wendy Ann) 175.00
    8" hp., BK, #775, 1965–1972 (Wendy Ann) 125.00
    8" hp., #775, BK & BKW, white ....145.00 up
    8" hp., straight leg, #0775, #575, 1973–1975, marked "Alex." 60.00
    8" hp., straight leg, #575, #549, 1976–1988, marked "Alexander" (1985–1987 white face)..........55.00
    10" hp., 1962–1963 (Cissette) ....1,200.00 up
INDIAN BOY* 8" hp., BK, #720, 1966 only, Americana Series (Wendy Ann) 375.00
INDIAN GIRL* 8" hp., BK, #721, 1966 only, Americana Series (Wendy Ann) 400.00
INDONESIA 8" hp., BK, #779, 1970–1972 (Wendy Ann)..165.00
    8" hp., straight leg, #779, #0779, #579, 1972–1975, marked "Alex." 60.00
    8" hp., straight leg, #579, 1976–1988, marked "Alexander" 55.00
    BK, with Maggie Mixup face..175.00
INGALLS, LAURA 14", #1531, 1989–1991, Classic Series, burnt orange dress/blue pinafore (Mary Ann)..80.00
INGRES 14" plastic/vinyl, #1567, 1987 only, Fine Arts Series (Mary Ann) 70.00
IRIS 10" hp., #1112, 1987–1988, pale blue (Cissette) 85.00
IRISH (IRELAND) 8" hp., BKW, #778, 1965 only (Wendy Ann) 175.00
    8" BK, #778, 1966–1972, long gown 125.00
    8" straight leg, #0778, #578, 1973–1975, marked "ALEX", long gown 60.00
    8" straight leg, #578, #551, 1976–1985, marked "Alexander"................................55.00
    8" straight leg, #551, 1985–1987, short dress, white face 55.00
    8" straight leg, #551, 1987–1992, marked "Alexander," short dress (Maggie) 52.00
ISOLDE 14", #1413, 1985–1986 only, Opera Series (Mary Ann)..................................75.00
ISRAEL 8" hp., BK, #768, 1965–1972 (Wendy Ann) 125.00
    8" hp., straight leg, #0768, 1973–1975, marked "Alex." 60.00
    8" hp., straight leg, #568, 1976–1989 (1985–1987 white face), marked "Alexander" 55.00
ITALY 8" hp., BKW, #393, 1961–1965 (Wendy Ann) 185.00
    8" hp., BK, #793, 1965–1972 ....125.00
    8" hp., straight leg, #0793, #593, 1973–1975, marked "ALEX." 60.00
    #593, 1985, white face 55.00
    8" straight leg, #593, #553, #524, 1976–1993, marked "Alexander" 55.00

* *Became* HIAWATHA *and* POCAHONTAS *in 1967.*

···➤ J ◄···

Please read "About Pricing" for additional information.

JACK & JILL   7" compo., 1938–1943 (Tiny Betty) ....each 265.00
   9" compo., 1939 only (Little Betty) ....each 285.00
   8" straight leg, (Jack - #455, #457. Jill - #456, #458), 1987–1992, Storybook Series (Maggie) ..each 52.00
JACKSON, SARAH   1979–1981, 2nd set Presidents' Ladies/First Ladies Series (Louisa) 100.00
JACQUELINE IN RIDING HABIT   1962 ....575.00
   In gown from cover of 1962 catalog 650.00
JACQUELINE   21" hp./vinyl arms, 1961–1962, street dress or suit 550.00
   Ballgown 650.00
   10" hp., 1962 only (Cissette) 425.00
JACQUELINE   1962, 1966–1967, exclusive in trunk with wardrobe ....1,500.00 up
JAMAICA   8" straight leg, #542, 1986–1988 (Wendy Ann) 75.00
JANIE   12" toddler, #1156, 1964–1966 only 300.00
   Ballerina, 1965 only 325.00
   14" baby, 1972–1973 ....55.00
   20" baby, 1972–1973 ....75.00
JAPAN   8" hp., BK, #770, 1968–1972 (Wendy Ann) 125.00
   8" hp., straight leg, #0770, #570, 1973–1975, marked "Alex." 60.00
   8" hp., straight leg, #570, 1976–1986, marked "Alexander" 55.00

10" JACQUELINE, 1962

Sitting: 12" JANIE, 1964. Standing: 12" ROZY, 1969 only.

8", #570, 1987–1991 (Maggie) 52.00

8" BK, #770, 1960's (Maggie Mixup) 165.00

8" hp., #526, reintroduced 1992–1993, white face (Wendy Ann) 60.00

JASMINE 10", #1113, 1987–1988, Portrette Series, burnt orange (Cissette) 78.00

JEANNIE WALKER 13–14" compo., 1940's 550.00

18" compo., 1940's ....685.00 up

JENNIFER'S TRUNK SET 14" doll, #1599, 1990 only 250.00

JESSICA 18" cloth/vinyl, 1990 only 95.00

JO (see Little Women)

JOANIE 36" plastic/vinyl, 1960–1961 ....365.00

36", 1960, nurse dressed in all white with black band on cap 385.00

36", 1961, nurse in colored uniform, all white pinafore and cap 385.00

JOHN 8", #440, 1993, Peter Pan Series, wears glasses 65.00

JOHN POWER'S MODELS 14" hp., 1952 only (Maggie & Margaret) ....1,400.00 up

18", 1952 only ....1,500.00 up

JONES, CASEY 8" hp., Americana Series, 1991–1992 only (Wendy Ann) 52.00

JOSEPHINE 12", #1335, 1980–1986, Portrait of History (Nancy Drew) 55.00

JOY 12", 1990, New England Collectors (see Special Events/Exclusives)

JOY NOEL 1993 (see Spiegels under Special Events/Exclusives)

JUDY 21" compo., 1945–1947 (Wendy Ann) ....2,300.00 up

21" hp./vinyl arms, 1962 only (Jacqueline) 1,700.00

JUGO-SLAV 7" compo., 1935–1937 (Tiny Betty) 250.00

JULIET 21" compo., 1945–1946, Portrait Series (Wendy Ann) ....2,300.00 up

18" compo., 1937–1940 (Wendy Ann) ....1,200.00 up

8" hp., #473, 1955 only (Wendy Ann) ....1,300.00 up

12" plastic/vinyl, 1978–1987, Portrait Children Series (Nancy Drew) 55.00

12", reintroduced 1991–1992, Romance Collection (Nancy Drew) 105.00

JUNE BRIDE 21" compo., 1939, 1946–1947, Portrait Series.................................2,000.00 up

36" JOANIE, 1960

Please read "About Pricing" for additional information.

KAREN 15–18" hp., 1948–1949 (Margaret)..750.00 up
KAREN BALLERINA 15" compo., 1946–1949 (Margaret)...700.00 up
   18–21", can be dressed in pink, yellow, blue, white, or lavender............................750.00 up
KATE GREENAWAY 7" compo., 1938–1943 (Tiny Betty)...285.00
   9" comp., 1936–1939 (Little Betty)..300.00
   16" cloth, 1936–1938..700.00
   13", 14", 15" compo., 1938–1943 (Princess Elizabeth)........................500.00–650.00
   18", 1938–1943...800.00
   24", 1938–1943..950.00 up
   14" vinyl, #1538, 1993, Classic Series..115.00
KATHLEEN TODDLER 23" rigid vinyl, 1959 only...100.00
KATIE (BLACK SMARTY) 12" plastic/vinyl, 1963 only 265.00
   12" (Black Janie), #1156, #1155, 1965 only..350.00
   12" hp., 1962 Anniversary doll for FAO Schwarz (Lissy)............................1,200.00 up
KATHY 15–18" hp., 1949–1951, has braids (Maggie)..750.00
KATHY BABY 13–15" vinyl, 1954–1956, has rooted or molded hair....................65.00–125.00
   11–13" vinyl, 1955–1956, has rooted or molded hair...65.00–125.00
   18–21", 1954–1956, has rooted or molded hair...100.00–150.00

12" KELLY, 1959
Mint condition, priced above book price.

11" vinyl, 1955–1956, doll has molded hair and comes with trousseau 125.00
21", 1954 only 165.00
21" & 25", 1955–1956 .... 125.00–200.00
KATHY CRY DOLLY 11–15" vinyl nurser, 1957–1958 .... 60.00–85.00
18", 21", 25" 75.00–125.00
KATHY TEARS 11", 15", 17" vinyl, 1959–1962, has closed mouth 50.00–85.00
19", 23", 26", 1959–1962 .... 100.00–150.00
12", 16", 19" vinyl, 1960–1961 (new face) 60.00–85.00
KEANE, DORIS Cloth, 1930's 675.00
9–11" compo., 1936–1937 (Little Betty) 285.00
KELLY 12" hp., 1959 only (Lissy) 450.00
15–16", 1958–1959 (Marybel) 400.00
16", 1959 only, in trunk/wardrobe .... 950.00 up
22", 1958–1959 .... 475.00
8" hp., #433, 1959, blue/white dress 365.00
KENNEDY, JACQUELINE 14", 1989–1990, 6th set Presidents' Ladies/First Ladies Series (Mary Ann) 100.00
KING 21" compo., 1942–1946 (Wendy Ann) 2,400.00
KITTEN 14–18" cloth/vinyl, 1962–1963 .... 35.00–75.00
24", 1961 only, has rooted hair 85.00
20" nurser, 1968 only, has cryer box, doesn't wet 75.00
20", 1985–1986 only, dressed in pink 85.00
KITTEN, LITTLEST (see Littlest Kitten)
KITTEN KRIES 20" cloth/vinyl, 1967 only 85.00
KITTEN, MAMA 18", 1963 only, same as "Lively" but also has cryer box 100.00
KITTEN, LIVELY 14", 18", 24", 1962–1963, knob moves head and limbs 100.00
KITTY BABY 21" compo., 1941–1942 .... 125.00
KLONDIKE KATE 10" hp., 1963 only, Portrette Series (Cissette) .... 1,200.00 up
KOREA 8" hp., BK, #772, 1968–1970 (Wendy Ann) 325.00
BKW & BK, #772, (Maggie Mixup) 350.00
#522, reintroduced 1988–1989 (Maggie Mixup) 80.00

10" GOLD RUSH, KLONDIKE KATE, and QUEEN

Please read "About Pricing" for additional information.

LADY BIRD 8", #438, 1988–1989, Storybook Series (Maggie)..85.00
LADY HAMILTON 20" hp./vinyl arms, 1957 only, Models Formal Series (Cissy)
    picture hat, blue gown w/shoulder shawl effect 850.00
    11" hp., 1957, pink silk gown, picture hat with roses (Cissette)...................................450.00
    21", #2182, 1968, beige lace over pink gown (Jacqueline) 575.00
    12" vinyl, #1338, 1984–1986, Portrait of History (Nancy Drew) 50.00
LADY IN RED 20", #1134, 1958 only, red taffeta (Cissy) 1,200.00
    10", 1990, Portrette Series (Cissette) 90.00
LADY IN WAITING 8" hp., #487, 1955 only (Wendy Ann) ....1,200.00 up
LADY LEE 8", #442, 1988 only, Storybook Series 85.00
LADY LOVELACE Cloth/felt, 1930's 600.00
LADY WINDERMERE 21" compo., 1945–1946 ....2,200.00 up
LAMARR, HEDY 17" hp., 1949 only (Margaret) ....1,400.00 up
LANE, HARRIET 1982–1984, 3rd set Presidents' Ladies/First Ladies Series (Mary Ann) 90.00
LAOS 8" straight leg, #525, 1987–1988 ....80.00
LAPLAND 8" hp., #537, 1993 ....54.00
LATVIA 8" straight leg, #527, 1987 only 90.00
LAUGHING ALLEGRA Cloth, 1932 ....650.00
LAURIE, LITTLE MEN 8" hp., BK, #781, #755, 1966–1972 (Wendy Ann)..................145.00
    Straight leg, #0755, #416, 1973–1975, marked "Alex." 60.00
    Check pants, marked "Alexander" 55.00
    Straight leg, #416, #410, 1976–1992 (1985–1987 white face) 50.00
    12" all hp., 1967 only (Lissy) 350.00
    12" plastic/vinyl, 1967–1988 (Nancy Drew) 65.00
LAURIE, PIPER 14" hp., 1950 only (Margaret) ....1,400.00 up
    21" hp., 1950 only ....1,600.00 up
LAZY MARY 7" compo., 1936–1938 (Tiny Betty) 265.00
LENA (see "River Boat")
LE PETITE BOUDOIR 1993 (see C.U. under Special Events/Exclusives)
LESLIE (BLACK POLLY) 17" vinyl, 1965–1971, in dress 400.00
    1966–1971, as bride 350.00
    1965–1971, in formal or ballgown 485.00
    In trunk with wardrobe ....900.00 up
    1966–1971, as ballerina 375.00
LETTY BRIDESMAID 7–8" compo., 1938–1940 (Tiny Betty) 275.00
LEWIS, SHARI 14", 1958–1959 ....400.00
    21", 1958–1959 ....600.00
LIESL (see "Sound of Music")
LIL CHRISTMAS COOKIE 8", #341, 1993, Americana Series 60.00
LIL CLARA AND THE NUTCRACKER 8", #480, 1993, Storyland Series 55.00
LILA BRIDESMAID 7–8" compo., 1938–1940 (Tiny Betty) 275.00
LILAC FAIRIE 21" porcelain, 1993, Portrait ballerina 310.00
LILIBET 16" compo., 1938 (Princess Elizabeth) ....650.00 up
LILY 10", #1114, 1987–1988, red/black (Cissette) 85.00
LINCOLN, MARY TODD 1982–1984, 3rd set Presidents' Ladies/First Ladies Series (Louisa) 150.00
LIND, JENNY 21" hp./vinyl arms, #2191, 1969, dressed in all pink, no trim (Jacqueline)..............1,500.00
    #2181, 1970, all pink with lace trim 1,500.00
    10", #1171, 1969, Portrette Series, all pink, no trim (Cissette) 600.00
    10", #1184, 1970, Portrette Series, pink with lace trim (Cissette) 600.00
    14" plastic/vinyl, #1491, #1490, 1970–1971, Portrait Children Series (Mary Ann) 500.00
LIND, JENNY & LISTENING CAT 14", #1470, 1970–1971, Portrait Children Series (Mary Ann)..............425.00

LION TAMER 8", #306, 1990, Americana Series (Wendy Ann) 75.00

LISSY 11½"–12" hp., 1956–1958, jointed knees & elbows 300.00

    1956–1958, as ballerina 325.00

    1956–1958, as bride ....350.00 up

    1956–1957, as bridesmaid ....500.00 up

    1958, dressed in formal...500.00 up

    1956–1958, in street dresses 300.00

    1956, in window box with wardrobe..1,400.00 up

    21", one-piece arm, pink tulle pleated skirt (Cissy) 1,000.00

    21", #2051, 1966, pink tiara (Coco) 2,300.00

    12" hp., 1957, jointed elbows & knees, in window box with wardrobe (Lissy)...................1,400.00 up

    12" hp., one-piece arms & legs in window box/wardrobe, 1959–1966 (Lissy) ....1,000.00 up

    Classics (see individuals, example: McGuffey Ana, Scarlett, Cinderella)

LISSY in box with wardrobe from 1956.
Priced above book price because of MIB condition.

LITTLE ANGEL 9" latex/vinyl, 1950–1957 ....100.00

LITTLE AUDREY Vinyl, 1954 only ....250.00 up

LITTLE BETTY 9–11" compo., 1935–1943, must be mint 300.00–400.00

LITTLE BITSEY 9" all vinyl nurser, 1967–1968 (Sweet Tears)...165.00

LITTLE BO PEEP (see Bo Peep, Little)

LITTLE BOY BLUE 7" compo., 1937–1939 (Tiny Betty)..285.00

LITTLE BUTCH 9" all vinyl nurser, 1967–1968 (Sweet Tears)..165.00

LITTLE CHERUB 11" compo., 1945–1946 ....165.00

    7" all vinyl, 1960 only 200.00

LITTLE COLONEL 8½–9" compo., closed mouth, 1935 (Betty) 465.00

    11–13" compo., closed mouth (Betty) 575.00–650.00

    17" compo., closed mouth (Betty) 850.00

    17", open mouth (Betty) 600.00–700.00

    18–23", open mouth 825.00

    26–27", open mouth ....975.00 up

LITTLE DEVIL 8" hp., Americana Series, 1992 ....55.00
LITTLE DORRIT 16" cloth, early 1930's, Dicken's character 650.00
LITTLE EDWARDIAN 8" hp., SL, SLW, #0200, 1953–1955, long dotted navy gown ....1,200.00 up
LITTLE EMILY 16" cloth, early 1930's, Dicken's character 650.00
LITTLE EMPEROR (see U.F.D.C. under Special Events/Exclusives)
LITTLE GENIUS 12–14" compo./cloth, 1935–1940, 1942–1946 ....120.00
    18–20" compo./cloth, 1935–1937, 1942–1946 ....135.00
   24–25", 1936–1940 ....125.00
   8" hp./vinyl, 1956–1962, nude (clean condition), good face color 275.00
     Dressed in cotton play dress 275.00
     In dressy, lacy outfit with bonnet 325.00
     Dressed in christening outfit 385.00
   Sewing or Gift Set, 1950's ....950.00 up
   7" vinyl, 1993, reintroduced doll with painted eyes 42.00
     Dressed in blue jumpsuit 42.00
     Dressed in pink lacy dress 42.00
     Extra packaged outfits ....each 25.00
LITTLE GODEY 8" hp., #491, 1953–1955 (Wendy Ann) ....1,200.00 up

Both are LITTLE COLONEL dolls from 1935.

15" LITTLE GENUIS, 1935–1940

LITTLE GRANNY   14" plastic/vinyl, #1431, 1966 only, floral gown (Mary Ann) 285.00
    14", #1430, 1966 only, pinstripe gown (also variations) (Mary Ann)...250.00
LITTLE JACK HORNER   7" compo., 1937–1943 (Tiny Betty) 265.00
LITTLE JUMPING JOAN   8", #487, 1989–1990, Storybook Series (Maggie Mixup)................................85.00
LITTLE LADY DOLL   8" hp., #1050, 1960 only, gift set, in mint condition (Maggie Mixup) ....450.00 up
    8" doll only 275.00
    21" hp., 1949, has braids & Colonial gown (Wendy Ann)..2,200.00
LITTLE LORD FAUNTLEROY   Cloth, 1930's 650.00
    13" compo., 1936–1937 (Wendy Ann) ....600.00 up
LITTLE MADELINE   8" hp., 1953–1954 (Madeline) ....650.00 up
LITTLE MAID   8" straight leg, #423, 1987–1988, Storybook Series (Wendy Ann) 90.00
LITTLE MELANIE   8" hp., #633, 1955–1956, (Wendy Ann) ....1,000.00 up
LITTLE MEN   15" hp., 1950–1952 (Margaret & Maggie) ....each 850.00
LITTLE MEN   Set with Tommy, Nat & Stuffy ....set 2,900.00
LITTLE MERMAID   10", #1145, 1992–1993, Portrette Series, green/blue outfit (Cissette) 105.00
LITTLE MINISTER   8" hp., #411, 1957 only (Wendy Ann) ....2,000.00 up
LITTLE MISS   8" hp., #489, 1989–1991 only, Storybook Series (Maggie Mixup) 75.00
LITTLE MISS GODEY   (see M.A.D.C. under Special Events/Exclusives)
LITTLE MISS MAGNIN   (see I. Magnin under Special Events/Exclusives)
LITTLE NANNIE ETTICOAT   Straight leg, #428, 1986–1988, Storybook Series 85.00
LITTLE NELL   16" cloth, early 1930's, Dickens character ....550.00 up
    14" compo., 1938–1940 (Wendy Ann) ....650.00 up
LITTLE SHAVER   10" cloth, 1940–1944 ....465.00 up
    7" cloth, 1940–1944 ....500.00
    15" cloth, 1940–1944 ....535.00
    22", 1940–1944 ....600.00 up
    12", 1941–1943 (see Baby Shaver)
    12" plastic/vinyl, 1963–1965, has painted eyes 300.00
LITTLE SOUTHERN BOY/GIRL   10" latex/vinyl, 1950–1951 ....each 100.00
LITTLE SOUTHERN GIRL   8" hp., #305, 1953 only (Wendy Ann)..1,200.00 up
LITTLE VICTORIA   7½"–8", #376, 1953–1954 only (Wendy Ann) ....1,100.00 up
LITTLE WOMEN   (Meg, Jo, Amy, Beth)
    16" cloth, 1930–1936 ....each 575.00 up
    7" compo., 1935–1944 (Tiny Betty) ....each 275.00
    9" compo., 1937–1940 (Little Betty) ....each 295.00
    13–15" compo., 1937–1946 (Wendy Ann) ....each 450.00–550.00
    14–15" hp., 1947–1956, plus "Marme" (Margaret & Maggie) ....each 450.00   set 1,800.00
    14–15" hp., BK, plus "Marme" (Margaret & Maggie) ....each 475.00   set 1,900.00
    14–15" "Amy" with loop curls, must have good face color (Margaret)....................................550.00
    7½–8" hp., SL, SLW, all #609, 1955, plus "Marme" (Wendy Ann) ....each 225.00   set 1,000.00
    8" hp., BKW, all #609, all #409, all #481, 1956–1959 (Wendy Ann) ....each 175.00   set   950.00
    8" BK, all #381, 1960–1963, (Wendy Ann) ....each 135.00   set   700.00
        #781, 1964–1971 ....each 135.00   set   700.00
        #7811 to #7815, 1972–1973 ....each 135.00   set   700.00
    8" straight leg, #411 to #415, 1974–1986 ....each 50.00   set   300.00
        #405 to #409, 1987–1990 ....each 50.00   set   300.00
        #411 to #415, 1991–1992 ....each 53.00   set   350.00
    11½–12" hp., jointed elbows & knees, 1957–1958 (Lissy) ....each 275.00   set 1,400.00
    11½–12" hp., one-piece arms & legs, 1959–1966 (Lissy) ....each 175.00   set 1,000.00
    12" plastic/vinyl, 1969–1982 (Nancy Drew) ....each 50.00   set   300.00
    12" plastic/vinyl, 1983–1989, new outfits (Nancy Drew) ....each 50.00   set   300.00
    12" set for Sears, 1989–1990 only (see Special Events/Exclusives)
    12", 1993, no "Marme" (Lissy)...each 105.00

LITTLEST KITTEN 8" vinyl, 1963, nude, clean, good face color ....165.00 up
   Dressed in lacy dress oufit with bonnet 250.00
   Dressed in christening outfit 265.00
   In sewing or gift set ....900.00 up
   Dressed in play attire 165.00
LIVELY KITTEN 14", 18", 24", 1962–1963, knob makes limbs and head move 100.00–145.00
LIVELY PUSSY CAT 14", 20", 24", 1966–1969, knob makes limbs and head move 100.00–150.00
LOLA AND LOLLIE BRIDESMAID 7" compo., 1938–1940 (Tiny Betty) ....each 250.00 up
LOLLIE BABY Rubber/compo, 1941–1942 ....95.00
LOOBY LOO 15½" hp., ca 1951–1954 ....850.00 up
LORD FAUNTLEROY 12", 1981–1983, Portrait Children (Nancy Drew) 60.00
LOUISA (see "Sound of Music")
LOVEY DOVE 19" vinyl baby, closed mouth, molded or rooted hair, 1958–1959 ....165.00
   19" hp./latex, 1950–1951 ....50.00–75.00
   12" all hp. toddler, 1948–1951 (Precious) ....375.00 up
   1951, dressed as "Ringbearer" ....450.00 up
   "Answer Doll" with lever in back to move head ....485.00 up
LUCINDA 12" plastic/vinyl, 1969–1970 (Janie) ....300.00 up
   14" plastic/vinyl, #1435, #1535, 1971–1982, blue gown (Mary Ann) 70.00
   14", #1535, 1983–1986, Classic Series, pink or peach gown (Mary Ann) 75.00
LUCK OF THE IRISH 8", #327, 1992–1993, Americana Series (Maggie Mixup) 53.00
LUCY 8" hp., #488, 1961 only, Americana Series, strip cotton/poke bonnet (Wendy Ann) .....2,200.00 up
LUCY BRIDE 14" hp., 1949–1950 (Margaret) 500.00
   17" hp., 1949–1950 (Margaret) 625.00
   16½" hp./vinyl arms, 1958 only (Elise) 350.00
   14" compo., 1937–1940 (Wendy Ann) 325.00
   17" compo., 1937–1940 (Wendy Ann) 425.00
   21" compo., 1942–1944, Portrait, extra make-up (Wendy Ann) 1,800.00
LUCY LOCKET 8" straight leg, #433, 1986–1988, Storybook Series 70.00

Please read "About Pricing" for additional information.

M.A.D.C. (Madame Alexander Doll Club) (see Special Events/Exclusives)
Madame Butterfly 10", 1990, Marshall Fields (see Special Events/Exclusives)
Madame Doll 21" hp./vinyl arms, 1966 only, pink brocade (Coco) ....2,400.00 up
    14" plastic/vinyl, #1460, #1561, 1967–1975, Classic Series (Mary Ann)............................400.00
Madame (Alexander) 21", 1984 only, one-piece skirt in pink 400.00
    21", 1985–1987, pink with overskirt that unsnaps 375.00
    21", 1988–1990, blue with full lace overskirt 325.00
    8", 1993 only, introduced mid-year (see Special Events/Exclusives)
Madame Pompadour 21" hp./vinyl arms, #2197, 1970, pink lace overskirt (Jacqueline) 1,300.00
Madelaine 14" compo., 1940–1942 (Wendy Ann)..600.00
    17–18" hp., 1949–1953, must be mint ....950.00 up
    18" hp./vinyl, 1961 only, short dress..700.00 up
       Dressed in ballgown ....900.00 up
    8" hp., 1954, FAO Schwarz special ....650.00 up
Madelaine Du Bain 11" compo., closed mouth, 1937 (Wendy Ann)....................................465.00
    14" compo., 1938–1939 (Wendy Ann) 550.00
    17" compo., 1939–1941 (Wendy Ann) 675.00
    21" compo., 1939–1941 (Wendy Ann) 800.00
    14" hp., 1949–1951 (Maggie) ....950.00 up
Madeline 17–18" hp./jointed elbows & knees, 1950–1953 ....950.00 up
    18" hp., vinyl head, extra jointed body, 1961 only ....950.00 up
    16½" Kelly, 1964 (Mary Ann)..475.00
    In trunk/wardrobe, various years ....900.00 up
Madison, Dolly 1976–1978, 1st set Presidents' Ladies/First Ladies Series (Martha) 110.00

8" Maggie Mixup, 1960

MAGGIE 15" hp., 1948–1954 (Little Women only to 1956) 525.00

    17–18", 1949–1953 ....685.00

    20–21", 1948–1954 ....725.00

    22–23", 1949–1952 ....800.00

    17" plastic/vinyl, 1972–1973 only (Elise) 325.00

MAGGIE MIXUP 16½" hp./vinyl, 1960 only (Elise body) 400.00

    17" plastic/vinyl, 1961 only ....300.00 up

    8" hp., #600, #611, #617, #627, 1960–1961 ....450.00

    8" hp., #618, 1961, as angel 1,000.00

    8", #610, 1960–1961, dressed in overalls and has watering can 650.00

    8", #626, 1960–1961, dressed in skater outfit 550.00

    8", #634, 1960–1961, dressed in riding habit 550.00

    8", #593, 1960, dressed in roller skating outfit 500.00

    8", #598, #597, #596, 1960, wearing dresses or skirts/blouses ....450.00 up

MAGGIE TEENAGER 15–18" hp., 1951–1953 ....565.00 up

    23", 1951–1953 ....700.00 up

MAGGIE WALKER 15–18" hp., 1949–1953 ....500.00

    20–21", 1949–1953 ....685.00

    23–25", 1951–1953 (with Cissy face) 650.00

MAGNOLIA 21", #2297, 1977 only, multi-rows lace on pink gown 500.00

    21", #2251, 1988 only, yellow gown 325.00

21" MAGGIE WALKER, 1950

MAID MARIAN   8" hp., #492, 1989–1991 only, Storybook Series (Wendy Ann) 85.00
   21", 1992–1993, Portrait Series (Jacqueline)...310.00
MAID OF HONOR   18" compo., 1940–1944 (Wendy Ann)...850.00 up
   14" plastic/vinyl, #1592, 1988–1989, Classic Series, blue gown (Mary Ann) 75.00
MAJORETTE   14–17" compo., 1937–1938 (Wendy Ann)...850.00 up
   8" hp., #482, 1955 only, (Drum Majorette) (Wendy Ann)..950.00 up
   8", #314, 1991–1992 only, Americana Series, no baton 55.00
MAMA KITTEN   18", #402, 1963 only, knob moves head & limbs, cryer box 125.00
MAMMY   8", #402, 1989 only, Jubilee II set (black "round" face) 95.00
   8" hp., #635, 1991–1992 only, Scarlett Series (black Wendy Ann) 55.00
MANET   21", #2225, 1982–1983, light brown with dark brown pinstripes (Jacqueline).......................325.00
   14", #1571, 1986–1987, Fine Arts Series (Mary Ann) 70.00
MARCELLA DOLLS   13–24" compo., 1936 only, dressed in 1930's fashions ....each 650.00–900.00
MARCH HARE   Cloth/felt, mid 1930's 650.00
MARGARET ROSE   (see Princess)
MARGOT   10–11" hp., 1961 only, in formals (Cissette) ....400.00 up
   Street dresses, bathing suit, 1961 only 325.00
MARGOT BALLERINA   15–18", 1953–1955, dressed in various colored outfits (Margaret & Maggie) 625.00
   15–18" hp./vinyl arms, 1955 only (Cissy)..475.00
MARIA   (see Sound of Music)
MARIE ANTOINETTE   21", #2248, 1987–1988, multi-floral print with pink front insert (Jacqueline) 300.00
MARINE   14" compo., 1943–1944 (Wendy Ann)..750.00
MARIONETTES/TONY SARG   Compo., 1934–1940 ....285.00
   12" compo., Disney 350.00
MARM LIZA   21" compo., 1938, 1946 (Wendy Ann)...2,200.00
MARME   (see Little Women)
MARSHALL FIELDS   (see Special Events/Exclusives)
MARTA   (see Sound of Music)
MARTIN, MARY   14–17" hp., 1948–1952 (Margaret) 850.00–975.00
   14–17", 1948–1952, dressed in sailor suit or ballgown 900.00–1,200.00
MARY ANN   14" plastic/vinyl, 1965, tagged "Mary Ann", in red/white dress...............................200.00
   Dressed in skirt and sweater 200.00
   Ballerina...275.00 up
   14" ballerina, 1973–1982 ....150.00
MARYBEL   ("The doll that gets well.") 16" rigid vinyl, 1959–1965, doll only ....165.00 up
   1959, 1961, 1965, doll in case 350.00
   1960 only, doll in case with wardrobe..450.00
   1965 only, doll with very long straight hair, in case..500.00
MARY CASSATT BABY   14" cloth/vinyl, 1969–1970 ....135.00
   20", 1969–1970 ....200.00
   14" plastic/vinyl child, #1566, 1987 only, Fine Arts Series (Mary Ann) 75.00
MARY ELLEN   31" rigid vinyl, walker, 1954 only..650.00 up
   31" plastic/vinyl arms, 1955 only, non-walker with jointed elbows ....500.00 up
MARY ELLEN PLAYMATE   14" plastic/vinyl, 1965 only, Marshall Fields exclusive (Mary Ann)............325.00
   12", 1965, in case with wigs (Lissy) ....750.00 up
   17", 1965, exclusive 350.00
MARY GRAY   14" plastic/vinyl, #1564, 1988 only, Classic Series (Mary Ann) 70.00
MARY LENNOX   14", #1537, 1993, Classic Doll Series 105.00
MARY LOUISE   21" compo., 1938, 1946–1947 (Wendy Ann)..2,300.00
   18" hp., 1954 only, Me & My Shadow Series, burnt orange & olive green (Cissy) 1,600.00
   8" hp., #0035D, 1954 only, same as 18" Me & My Shadow Series (Wendy Ann).....................1,600.00
MARY, MARY   8" hp., BKW, BK, #751, 1965–1972, Storybook Series (Wendy Ann)........................125.00
   8" hp., straight leg, #0751, #451, 1973–1975, marked "Alex" 60.00

8" hp., straight leg, #451, 1976–1987, marked "Alexander" (1985–1987 white face) 55.00
8", #471, reintroduced 1992 only (Wendy Ann) 55.00
14", #1569, 1988–1991, Classic Series (Mary Ann) 70.00
MARY MINE   21" cloth/vinyl, 1977–1989 ....115.00
14" cloth/vinyl, 1977–1979 ....60.00
14", reintroduced 1989 ....60.00
MARY MUSLIN   19" cloth, 1951 only, pansy eyes 400.00
26", 1951 only 500.00
40", 1951 only 600.00
MARY, QUEEN OF SCOTS   21", #2252, 1988–1989 (Jacqueline) 400.00
MARY ROSE BRIDE   17" hp., 1951 only (Margaret) 600.00
16½", 1953, floral wreath circles near hem (Elise) 450.00
10", 1957, floral wreath (Cissette) 400.00
MARY SUNSHINE   15" plastic/vinyl, 1961 (Caroline) 385.00
MCELROY, MARY   1985–1987, 4th set Presidents' Ladies/First Ladies Series (Mary Ann) 80.00
MCGUFFEY ANA   16" cloth, 1934–1936 ....700.00
7" compo., 1935–1939 (Tiny Betty) 290.00
9" compo., 1935–1939 (Little Betty) 325.00
15" compo., 1935–1937 (Betty) 625.00
13" compo., 1938 (Wendy Ann) 700.00
11", 1937–1939, has closed mouth 650.00
11–13" compo., 1937–1944 (Princess Elizabeth) 500.00–625.00
14–16" compo., 1937–1944 (Princess Elizabeth) 525.00–700.00

**9" MCGUFFEY ANA from 1939.
Above book price due to condtion.**

**Cloth MCGUFFEY ANA from 1936.
Hat and coat are missing.**

17–20" compo., 1937–1943 (Princess Elizabeth)..700.00–800.00
21–25" compo., 1937–1942 (Princess Elizabeth)..800.00–950.00
28" compo., 1937–1939 (Princess Elizabeth)..1,00.00
17" compo., 1948–1949 (Margaret)...800.00
14½" compo., 1948, wears coat, hat & muff 750.00
18", 25", 31", 1955–1956, has flat feet (Cissy)..485.00–800.00
21" hp., 1948–1950 (Margaret)..900.00
12" hp., 1963 only (Lissy) ....1,200.00 up
8" hp., #616, 1956 only (Wendy Ann)..650.00
8" hp., #788, #388, 1963–1965 ("American Girl" in 1962–1963) 400.00
8", #496, 1990–1991 only, Storybook Series (Wendy Ann) 55.00
29" cloth/vinyl, 1952 only (Barbara Jane) 565.00
14" plastic/vinyl, #1450, 1968–1969, Classic Series, wears plaid dress/eyelet apron (Mary Ann) ...125.00
14" plastic/vinyl, #1525, 1977–1986, Classic Series, wears plaid dress (Mary Ann) 70.00
14" plastic/vinyl, #1526, 1987–1988, mauve stripe pinafore, Classic Series (Mary Ann) 70.00
McKee, Mary 1985–1987, 4th set Presidents' Ladies/First Ladies Series (Mary Ann) 80.00
McKinley, Ida 1988, 5th set Presidents' Ladies/First Ladies Series (Louisa) 70.00
Medici, Catherine de 21" porcelain, 1990–1991 ....525.00
Meg (see "Little Women")
Melanie 21" compo., 1945–1947 (Wendy Ann)...2,200.00 up
21" hp./vinyl arms, 1961, lace bodice & overdress over satin (Cissy) ....800.00 up
21", #2050, 1966, blue gown with wide lace down sides (Coco) 2,400.00
1967, #2173, blue dress with white rick-rack around hem ruffle (Jacqueline) 600.00

21" Portrait Melanie from 1946.

1968, #2181, blue dress with white trim 475.00
1969, #2193, blue gown, white trim, multi-rows of lace, bonnet 475.00
1970, #2196, white gown with red ribbon trim 450.00
1971, #2162, blue gown, white sequin trim..425.00
1974, #2195, white gown, red jacket and bonnet 525.00
1979–1980, #2220, white dotted swiss gown with pink trim 375.00
1981, pink nylon with blue ribbon 350.00
1989, #2254, all orange with lace shawl 350.00
10", #1173, 1968–1969, pink multi-tiered skirt (Cissette) 450.00
10", #1182, 1970, yellow multi-tiered skirt 450.00
10", 1989 only, two-toned peach dress with lace (Cissette) 95.00
8" hp., #633, 1955–1956 (Wendy Ann)..1,000.00
12", 1987 only, Portrait Children Series, aqua green gown, brown trim (Nancy Drew)................80.00
10", #1101, 1989 only, Jubilee II, all royal blue dress with black trim (Cissette) 95.00
8", #627, 1990, Scarlett Series, lavender/lace (Wendy Ann) 70.00
8", #628, 1992, peach gown/bonnet with lace 57.00
MELINDA   10" hp., 1968, blue gown with white trim (Cissette) 400.00
1970, yellow multi-tiered lace skirt...400.00
22", #1912, 1962 only, wears white organdy dress with red trim 425.00
14", 16", 22" plastic/vinyl, 1962–1963, dressed in cotton dress 400.00
14", 16", 22" plastic/vinyl, 1963, dressed in party dress 350.00–500.00
14", 1963 only, as ballerina ....350.00 up

**11" MICHAEL with bear
from Peter Pan Series, 1969.**

**30" MIMI, above book price.
Mint condition with tags.**

MELODY AND FRIEND   25" and 8" (see Special Events/Exclusives)
MERRY ANGEL   8", 1991, Spiegels (see Special Events/Exclusives)
METROPLEX DOLL CLUB   (see Special Events/Exclusives)
MEXICO   7" compo., 1936 (Tiny Betty) 265.00
   9" compo., 1938–1939 (Little Betty) 285.00
   8" hp., BKW, #776, 1964–1965 (Wendy Ann) 175.00
   8" hp., BK, #776, 1965–1972 ....130.00
   8" straight leg, #0776, 1973–1975, marked "ALEX" 60.00
   8" straight leg, #576, #550, #520, 1976–1991, marked "Alexander" (1985–1987 white face) 55.00
   1985, #550, white face 60.00
MICHAEL   11" plastic/vinyl, 1969 only (Janie) 365.00
   With teddy bear, mint condition 475.00
   8", #468, 1992–1993, Storybook Series (Peter Pan set) (Wendy Ann) 52.00
MIDNIGHT   21", #2256, 1990, dark blue/black (Jacqueline) 300.00
MILLER'S DAUGHTER   14" with 8" RUMPLESTILKINS, #1569, 1993, limited to 3,000 sets 260.00
MILLY   17" plastic/vinyl, 1968 only (Polly) 500.00
MIMI   30", hp. in 1961 only, multi-jointed body, dressed in formal 950.00
   Dressed in romper suit/skirt 600.00
   Dresed in Tyrolean outfit 1,000.00
   Dressed in slacks, stripe top, straw hat 600.00
   Dressed in red sweater, plaid skirt 600.00
   21" hp./vinyl arms, #2170, 1971, vivid pink cape & trim on white gown (Jacqueline) 650.00
   14", #1411, 1983–1986, Opera Series (Mary Ann) 85.00
MINISTER, LITTLE   8" hp., #411, 1957 only 1,900.00
MISS AMERICA   14" compo., 1941–1943, holds flag ....650.00 up
MISS LEIGH   8", 1989, made for C.U. Gathering (see Special Events/Exclusives)
MISS LIBERTY   10" (see M.A.D.C. under Special Events/Exclusives)
MISS MAGNIN   1991 (see I. Magnin under Special Events/Exclusives)
MISS MUFFETT   8" hp., BK, #752, 1965–1972, Storybook Series (Wendy Ann) 125.00
   8" straight leg, #0752, #452, 1973–1975, marked "Alex" 60.00
   8" straight leg, #452, 1976–1986 (1985–1986 white face), marked "Alexander" (Wendy Ann) 55.00
   8" straight leg, #452, 1987–1988 (Maggie) 60.00
   8", #493, 1993, Storybook Series 65.00
MISS UNITY   1991, made for U.F.D.C. (see Special Events/Exclusives)
MISS U.S.A.   8" hp., BK, #728, 1966–1968, Americana Series (Wendy Ann) 325.00
MISS VERMONT   8", 1990 (see Enchanted Doll House under Special Events/Exclusives)
MISS VICTORY   20" compo., 1944–1946, magnets in hands (Princess Elizabeth) ....750.00 up
MISTRESS MARY   7" compo., 1937–1941 (Tiny Betty) 275.00
MOLLY   14", #1561, 1988 only, Classic Series (Mary Ann) 80.00
MOLLY COTTONTAIL   Cloth/felt, 1930's 650.00
MOMBO   8" hp., #481, 1955 only (Wendy Ann) ....1,000.00 up
MOMMY & ME   14" compo., 1948–1949 (Margaret) ....900.00 up
MOMMY'S PET   14–20", 1977–1986 ....85.00 up
MONET   21", #2245, 1984–1985, black & white check gown with red jacket (Jacqueline) 325.00
MONROE, ELIZABETH   1976–1978, 1st set Presidents' Ladies/First Ladies Series (Mary Ann) 110.00
MOSS ROSE   14", #1559, 1991 only, Classic Series (Louisa) 155.00
MORISOT   21", #2236, 1985–1986 only, lime green gown with white lace (Jacqueline) 325.00
MOROCCO   8" hp., BK, #762, 1968–1970 (Wendy Ann) 375.00
MOTHER & ME   14–15" and 9" compo., 1940–1943 (Wendy Ann & Little Betty) ....850.00 up
MOTHER GOOSE   8" straight leg, #427, #459, 1986–1992, Storybook Series (Wendy Ann) 55.00
MOTHER GOTHEL   8", #1539, limited to 3,000 sets, comes in set with 14" RAPUNZEL doll ....set 2,600.00
MOTHER HUBBARD   8", #439, #459, 1988–1989, Storyland Series (Wendy Ann) 60.00
MOUSKETEER   1991 (see Disney under Special Events/Exclusives)

MR. O'HARA 8", #638, 1993, Scarlett Series (Wendy Ann) 57.00
MRS. BUCK RABBIT Cloth/felt, mid-1930's 625.00
MRS. DARLING 10", 1993, Peter Pan Series (Cissette) 105.00
MRS. MARCH HARE Cloth/felt, mid-1930's 625.00
MRS. O'HARA 8", #638, 1992–1993, Scarlett Series (Wendy Ann) 57.00
MRS. QUACK-A-FIELD Cloth/felt, mid-1930's 650.00
MRS. SNOOPIE Cloth/felt, 1940's 650.00
MUFFIN 19" cloth, 1966 only 95.00
    14", 1963–1977 ....95.00
    14" cloth, 1965 only, sapphire eyes 75.00
    14" black cloth, 1965–1966 only 95.00
    14" cloth, 1966–1970, cut slanted blue eyes 55.00
    14 cloth, eyes like sideward commas 55.00
    12" all vinyl, 1989–1990 (Janie)...75.00
    12", 1990–1992, in trunk/wardrobe 185.00
MY DOLL HOUSE (see Special Events/Exclusives)
MY LITTLE SWEETHEART (see Child At Heart under Special Events/Exclusives)

7" MISTRESS MARY, 1937

Please read "About Pricing" for additional information.

Nan McDare Cloth/felt, 1940's 650.00
Nana 6" dog with bonnet, #441, 1993, Peter Pan Series 44.00
Nana/Governess 8" hp., #433, 1957 only (Wendy Ann) ....1,900.00 up
Nancy Ann 17–18" hp., 1950 only ....875.00 up
Nancy Dawson 8", #441, 1988–1989, Storybook Series, (Maggie) 75.00
Nancy Drew 12" plastic/vinyl, 1967 only, Literature Series 400.00
Nancy Jean 8", 1990, Belk's (see Special Events/Exclusives)
Napoleon 12", #1330, 1980–1986, Portraits of History (Nancy Drew) 70.00
Nat (Little Men) 15" hp., 1952 (Maggie) ....850.00 up
Natasha #2255, 21", 1989–1990, brown & paisley brocade (Jacqueline) 355.00
Nashville Skater #1, 1991 (see C.U under Special Events/Exclusives)
    #2, 1992 (see C.U under Special Events/Exclusives)
National Velvet 12", 1991 only, Romance Series, no riding crop (Nancy Drew) 80.00
Neiman-Marcus 8", 1990 (see Special Events/Exclusives)
Nelson, Lord 12" vinyl, 1336, 1984–1986, Portraits of History (Nancy Drew) 60.00
Netherland Boy Formerly "Dutch" (Wendy Ann)
    8" hp., straight leg, #577, 1974–1975, marked "Alex" 60.00
    8" hp., straight leg, #577, 1976–1989, marked "Alexander" (1985–1987 white face) 55.00
Netherland Girl 8" hp., #591, #525, 1974–1992 (Wendy Ann) 55.00
New England Collector Society (see Special Events/Exclusives)

14" Nina Ballerina, 1950

NICOLE 10", #1139, 1989–1990, Portrette Series, black/off white outfit (Cissette) 85.00

NIGHTINGALE, FLORENCE 14", #1598, 1986–1987, Classic Series 70.00

NINA BALLERINA 7" compo., 1940 (Tiny Betty) 285.00

    9" compo., 1939–1941 (Little Betty) 325.00

    14" hp., 1949–1951 (Margaret) ....600.00 up

    17", 1949–1951 ....675.00

    15" hp., 1951, came in various colors all years (Margaret) 675.00

    19", 1949–1950 ....850.00 up

    23", 1951 ....850.00

NOD (see Dutch Lullaby)

NOEL 12", 1989–1991, New England Collectors Society (see Special Events/Exclusives)

NORMANDY 7" compo., 1935–1938 (Tiny Betty) 245.00

NORWAY 8" hp., BK, #584, 1968–1972 (Wendy Ann) 125.00

    8" straight leg, #584, 1973–1975, marked "Alex." 60.00

    8" straight leg, #584, 1976–1987, marked "Alexander" (1985–1987 white face) 55.00

NORWEGIAN 7–8" compo., 1936–1940 (Tiny Betty) 245.00

    9" compo., 1938–1939 (Little Betty) 275.00

NURSE 7" compo., 1936–1939 (Tiny Betty) 300.00

    13–15" compo., 1936–1940 (Betty) 550.00

    15" compo., 1939, 1943 (Princess Elizabeth) 525.00

    8" hp., #563, 1956 only, all white (Wendy Ann) ....400.00 up

        #429, 1961, all white dress, comes with baby ....450.00 up

    8" BKW, BK, #329, #460, #660, #624, 1962–1965, wears stripe dress, comes with baby 550.00

    8" hp., #308, #306, 1990–1991 only, Americana Series,

        blue/white striped dress, white pinafore & cap 60.00

Please read "About Pricing" for additional information.

O'BRIEN, MARGARET   14½" compo., 1946–1948 ....750.00
  17", 18", 19" compo., 1946–1948 ....900.00–1,000.00
  21–24" compo., 1946–1948 ....1,000.00–1,300.00
  14½" hp., 1949–1951 ....950.00
  17–18" hp., 1949–1951 ....1,100.00
  21–22" hp., 1949–1951 ....1,350.00
OKTOBERFEST 1993 (see C.U. under Special Events/Exclusives)
OLD FASHIONED GIRL   13" compo., 1945–1947 (Betty) ....475.00 up
  20" hp., 1948 only (Margaret) ....800.00 up
  14" hp., 1948 only (Margaret) 650.00
OLIVER TWIST   16" cloth, 1934, Dicken's character 650.00
  7" compo., 1935–1936 (Tiny Betty) 285.00
  8", #472, 1992 only, Storyland Series (Wendy Ann) 52.00
OLIVER TWISTAIL   Cloth/felt, 1930's 650.00
OPENING NIGHT   10", #1126, 1989 only, Portrette, gold sheath and overshirt (Cissette) 80.00
OPHELIA   12", 1992, Romance Collection (Nancy Drew) 120.00
  12", 1993 (Lissy) 115.00
ORCHARD PRINCESS   21" compo., 1939, 1946–1947 (Wendy Ann) ....2,200.00 up
ORPHANT ANNIE   14" plastic/vinyl, #1480, 1965–1966 only, Literature Series (Mary Ann) 375.00
  #1485, 1965 only, in window box with wardrobe ....850.00 up

21" MARGARET O'BRIEN, 1946
Above book price due to mint condition.

Please read "About Pricing" for additional information.

PAKISTAN 8" hp., #532, 1993 ....54.00
PAMELA 12" hp., 1962–1963 only, takes wigs (Lissy) ....doll only 400.00 up
   In case or window box, 1962–1963 ....1,000.00 up
   12" plastic/vinyl, 1969–1971 (Nancy Drew) ....doll only 175.00
   In case, 1969 ....450.00 up
PAN AMERICAN–POLLERA 7" compo., 1936–1938 (Tiny Betty) 285.00
PANAMA 8", #555, 1985–1987 ....80.00
PANDORA 8", 1991 (see Dolls 'n Bearland under Special Events/Exclusives)
PARLOUR MAID 8" hp., #579, 1956 only (Wendy Ann) ....1,500.00 up
PATCHITY PAM & PEPPER 15" cloth, 1965–1966 ....125.00
PATTERSON, MARTHA JOHNSON 1982–1984, 3rd set Presidents' Ladies/First Ladies Series (Martha) 90.00
PATTY 18" plastic/vinyl, 1965 only 350.00
PATTY PIGTAILS 14" hp., 1949 only (Margaret) ....850.00 up
PAULETTE 10", #1128, 1989–1990 only, Portrette, dressed in pink velvet (Cissette) 90.00
PEARL (JUNE) 10", #1150, 1992 only, Birthstone Collection, white/silver flapper doll 64.00
PEASANT 7" compo., 1936–1937 (Tiny Betty) 245.00
   9" compo., 1938–1939 (Little Betty) 275.00
PEGGY BRIDE 14–18" hp., 1950–1951 (Margaret) 525.00–600.00
   21" hp., 1950 ....675.00
PENNY 34" cloth/vinyl, 1951 only ....500.00 up
   42", 1951 only 675.00
   7" compo., 1938–1940 (Tiny Betty) 265.00
PERSIA 7" compo., 1936–1938 (Tiny Betty) 285.00
PERU 8", #556, 1986–1987 ....80.00
   8" hp., #531, 1993 (Wendy Ann) 54.00
PERUVIAN BOY 8" hp., BK, #770, 1965–1966 (Wendy Ann) 425.00
   8" hp., BKW, #770 ....500.00
PETER PAN 15" hp., 1953–1954 (Margaret) ....950.00 up
   8" hp., #310, 1953–1954 (Wendy Ann) ....1,100.00 up
   8" hp., #465, reintroduced 1991–1992, Storyland Series (Wendy Ann) 55.00
   14" plastic/vinyl, #1410, 1969 only (Mary Ann) 400.00
   1969 only, complete set of 4 dolls (Peter, Michael, Wendy, Tinkerbelle)........................1,500.00
PHILIPPINES 8" straight leg, #554, 1986–1987 ....75.00
   1987, #531, dressed in yellow gown 85.00
PICNIC DAY 18" hp., 1953 only, Glamour Girl Series (Margaret) ....1,400.00 up
PIERCE, JANE 1982–1984, 3rd set Presidents' Ladies/First Ladies Series (Mary Ann) 90.00
PIERROT CLOWN 8" hp., #561, 1956 only (Wendy Ann) 1,200.00
   14", #1558, 1991–1992, Classic Series (Mary Ann) 80.00
PILGRIM 7" compo., 1935–1938 (Tiny Betty) 265.00
PINKIE 12" plastic/vinyl, 1975–1987, Portrait Children (Nancy Drew) 50.00
PINKY 16" cloth, 1940's 550.00
   23" compo./cloth baby, 1937–1939 ....185.00
   13–19" vinyl baby, #3561, #5461, 1954 only, one-piece vinyl body and legs 65.00–95.00
PINOCCHIO 8", #477, 1992–1993, Storyland Series (Wendy Ann) 55.00
PIP All cloth, early 1930's, Dickens character 700.00
   7" compo., 1935–1936 (Tiny Betty) 300.00
PITTY PAT 16" cloth, 1950's 425.00
PITTY PAT CLOWN 1950's 450.00
PLAYMATES 29" cloth, 1940's ....450.00 up
POCAHONTAS 8" hp., BK, #721, 1967–1970, Americana & Storyland Series (Wendy Ann) 475.00
   8" hp., #318, reintroduced 1991–1992 only, Americana Series (Wendy Ann) 55.00

POLISH (POLAND) 8" hp., BKW, #780, 1964–1965 (Wendy Ann) 175.00
    8" BKW, #780, 1965 only (Maggie Mixup) 200.00
    8" hp., BK, #780, 1965–1972 ....125.00
    8" hp., straight leg, #0780, #580, 1973–1975, marked "ALEX." 60.00
    8" straight leg, #580, 1976–1988 (1985–1987 white face), marked "Alexander" 55.00
    7" compo., 1935–1936 (Tiny Betty) 245.00
    8", #523, reintroduced 1992–1993 (Maggie Mixup) 54.00
POLK, SARAH 1979–1981, 2nd set Presidents' Ladies/First Ladies Series (Martha) 90.00
POLLERA (PAN AMERICAN) 7" compo., 1936–1937 (Tiny Betty) 275.00
POLLY 17" plastic/vinyl, 1965 only, dressed in ballgown 425.00
    Dressed in street dress 375.00
    Dressed as ballerina 325.00
    Dressed as bride 325.00
    1965 only, came in trunk with wardrobe ....900.00 up
POLLY FLINDERS 8", #443, 1988–1989, Storybook Series (Maggie) 85.00
POLLY PIGTAILS 14½" hp., 1949–1951 (Maggie) 700.00
    17–17½", 1949–1951 ....900.00
    8" hp., 1990 (see M.A.D.C. under Special Events/Exclusives)
POLLY PUT KETTLE ON 7" compo., 1937–1939 (Tiny Betty) 245.00
POLLYANA 16" rigid vinyl, 1960–1961, marked "1958" (Marybel) 425.00
    Dressed in formal 550.00
    22", 1960–1961 ....500.00
    14", #1588, 1987–1988, Classic Series (Mary Ann) 70.00
    8", #474, 1992, Storyland Series (Maggie Mixup) 65.00
POODLES 14–17", 1940's, standing or sitting, named "Ivy" ....250.00 up
POOR CINDERELLA (see Cinderella)

17" POLLY PIGTAILS, 1949

POPPY   9" early vinyl, 1953 only, orange organdy dress & bonnet 100.00
PORTRAIT ELISE   17" plastic/vinyl, 1972–1973 ....175.00
PORTUGAL   8" hp., BK, #785, 1968–1972 (Wendy Ann) 125.00
    8" straight leg, #0785, #585, 1973–1975, marked "Alex." 60.00
    8" straight leg, #585, #537, 1976–1987, marked "Alexander" 55.00
    8", #537, 1986, white face 60.00
    8" hp., #535, 1993 ....54.00
POSEY PET   15" cloth, 1940's, plush rabbit or other animals 575.00
PRECIOUS   12" compo./cloth baby, 1937–1940 ....135.00
    12" all hp. toddler, 1948–1951 ....365.00 up
PREMIER DOLLS   8", 1990–1991 (see Special Events/Exclusives)
PRESIDENTS' LADIES/FIRST LADIES
    1st set, 1976–1978 ....110.00 singles   700.00 set
    2nd set, 1979–1981 ....90.00 singles   550.00 set
    3rd set, 1982–1984 ....90.00 singles   550.00 set
    4th set, 1985–1987 ....80.00 singles   475.00 set
    5th set, 1988 ....70.00 singles   450.00 set
    6th set, 1989–1990 ....100.00 singles   600.00 set
PRINCE CHARLES   8" hp., #397, 1957 only (Wendy Ann) ....575.00 up
PRINCE CHARMING   16–17" compo., 1947 (Margaret) 850.00
    14–15" hp., 1948–1950 (Margaret) 800.00
    17–18" hp., 1948–1950 (Margaret) 950.00

Some of the dolls from the first set of
PRESIDENTS' LADIES/FIRST LADIES

21" hp., 1949–1951 (Margaret) 1,000.00
12", 1990–1991, Romance Collection (Nancy Drew) 90.00
8", #479, 1993, Storybook Series, royal blue/gold outfit 75.00
PRINCE PHILLIP 17–18" hp., 1953 only, Beaux Arts Series (Margaret) 1,200.00
21", 1953 only 1,400.00
PRINCESS 12", 1990–1991 only, Romance Collection (Nancy Drew) 92.00
14", #1537, 1990 - Mary Ann; 1991 - Jennifer, Classic Series 150.00
20" hp., 1955 only, Child's Dream Comes True Series (Cissy) ....775.00 up
PRINCESS ALEXANDRIA 24" cloth/compo., 1937 only ....200.00 up
PRINCESS ANN 8" hp., #396, 1957 only (Wendy Ann) ....600.00 up
PRINCESS BUDIR AL-BUDOR 8", #483, 1993, Storybook Series 75.00
PRINCESS DOLL 13–15" compo., 1940–1942 (Princess Elizabeth) ....600.00 up
24" compo., 1940–1942 (Princess Elizabeth) ....800.00 up
PRINCESS ELIZABETH 7" compo., 1937–1939 (Tiny Betty) 300.00
8", 1937, with Dionne head 275.00
9–11" compo., 1937–1941 (Little Betty) 325.00–375.00
13" compo., 1937–1941, with closed mouth, ...500.00 up
14" compo., 1937–1941 ....500.00 up
15" compo., open mouth ....525.00 up
18–19" compo., 1937–1941, open mouth 650.00
24" compo., 1938–1939, open mouth ....800.00 up
28" compo., 1938–1939, open mouth ....950.00 up
PRINCESS FLAVIA (ALSO VICTORIA) 21" compo., 1939, 1946–1947 (Wendy Ann) ....2,300.00 up
PRINCESS MARGARET ROSE 15–18" compo., 1937–1938 (Princess Elizabeth) ....1,200.00 up
21" compo., 1938 ....965.00
14–18" hp., 1949–1953 (Margaret) ....775.00 up
18" hp., 1953 only, Beaux Art Series, pink taffeta gown & tiara (Margaret) ....1,400.00 up
PRINCESS ROSETTA 21" compo., 1939, 1946–1947 (Wendy Ann) 2,200.00
PRISCILLA 18" cloth, mid 1930's 625.00
7" compo., 1935–1938 (Tiny Betty) 275.00
8" hp., BK, #729, 1965–1970, Americana & Storybook Series (Wendy Ann) 385.00
PRISSY 8", #630, 1990 only, Scarlett Series (Wendy Ann) 65.00
8", #637, reintroduced 1992–1993 ....50.00
PROM QUEEN (see M.A.D.C. under Special Events/Exclusives)
PUDDIN' 14–21" cloth/vinyl, 1966–1975 ....85.00
14–18", 1987 ....75.00
14–21", 1990–1993 ....95.00–125.00
PUMPKIN 22" cloth/vinyl, 1967–1976 ....125.00
22", 1976 only, with rooted hair 145.00
PUSSY CAT Cloth/vinyl, white dolls:
14", 1965–1985 ....75.00
14", 1987–1993 ....60.00–105.00
14", 1966, 1968, in trunk/trousseau ....500.00 up
18", 1989–1993 ....95.00–115.00
20", 1965–1984, 1987–1988 ....95.00 up
24", 1965–1985 ....70.00–135.00
Cloth/vinyl, black dolls:
14", 1970–1976 ....75.00
14", 1984–1993 ....95.00
20", 1976–1983 ....110.00
PUSSY CAT, LIVELY 14", 20", 24", 1966–1969 only, knob makes head & limbs move 175.00

Please read "About Pricing" for additional information.

QUEEN   18" hp., 1953 only, Beaux Arts Series, white gown,
   velvet long cape trimmed with fur (Margaret) 1,600.00
   18" hp., 1953 only, Glamour Girl Series, same gown/tiara as above but no cape (Margaret).......1,000.00
   18" hp., 1954 only, Me & My Shadow Series, white gown, short orlon cape (Margaret) 1,600.00
   8" hp., 1954, #0030C, #597, Me & My Shadow Series,
   orlon cape attached to purple robe, (Wendy Ann) 1,500.00
   8", #499, 1955 only, scarlet velvet robe ....1,000.00 up
   10" hp., #971, #879, #842, #763, 1957–1958, 1960–1961, gold gown with blue ribbon 450.00
   #742, #765, 1959, 1963, white gown with blue ribbon 465.00
   #1186, #1187, 1972–1973, white gown with red ribbon 385.00
   1959, in trunk with wardrobe ....1,200.00 up
   14", #1536, 1990 only, Classic Series (Louisa, Jennifer) 950.00
   20" hp./vinyl arms, 1955, Dream Come True Series, white brocade gown (Cissy) 875.00
   1957, Fashion Parade Series, white gown 875.00
   1958, 1961–1963 (1958 - Dolls To Remember Series), gold gown 825.00
   18", 1963 only, white gown with red ribbon (Elise) ....750.00 up
   With Marybel head ....775.00 up

10" QUEEN PORTRETTE, 1960–1963

18" vinyl, same as 1965 (21" with rooted hair, 1966 only),
gold brocade gown, rare doll (Elise) ....1,200.00 up
#2150, 21" hp./vinyl arms, 1965, gold brocade gown (Jacqueline) ....950.00 up
1968, gold gown 1,000.00
QUEEN ALEXANDRINE 21" compo., 1939–1941 (Wendy Ann) 2,200.00
QUEEN CHARLOTTE 10", 1991 (see M.A.D.C. under Special Events/Exclusives)
QUEEN ELIZABETH I 10", 1990 (see My Doll House under Special Events/Exclusives)
QUEEN ELIZABETH II 8", 1992 only (mid-year issue), commemorating reign's 40th anniversary 135.00
QUEEN OF HEARTS 8" straight leg, #424, 1987–1990, Storybook Series (Wendy Ann)..........................85.00
10", 1992, Disney, #3 Annual Showcase of Dolls (see Special Events/Exclusives)
QUEEN ISABELLA 8" hp., #329, 1992 only, Americana Series 80.00
QUINTUPLETS (FISHER QUINTS) Hp., 1964, (Genius)...set 500.00
QUIZ-KINS 8" hp., 1953, bald head, in romper only (Wendy Ann)..475.00 up
1953–1954, as groom ....425.00 up
1953–1954, as bride 475.00
1953–1954, girl with wig, ...550.00
1953, girl without wig, in romper suit 450.00

7½" QUIZ-KIN, 1953–1954

Please read "About Pricing" for additional information.

RACHEL/RACHAEL 8", 1989 (see Belk's under Special Events/Exclusives)
RANDOLPH, MARTHA 1976–1978, 1st set First Ladies/Presidents' Ladies Series (Louisa) 110.00
RAPUNZEL 10", #M31, 1989–1992 only, Portrette Series, gold velvet (Cissette) 105.00
    14", #1539, 1993, Doll Classics, limited to 3,000, comes with 8" "Mother Gothel" 275.00
REBECCA 14–17", 21" compo., 1940–1941 (Wendy Ann) .... 500.00–1,000.00 up
    14" hp., 1948–1949 (Margaret) .... 800.00 up
    14" plastic/vinyl, #1485, 1968–1969, Classic Series, two-tiered skirt in pink (Mary Ann) 200.00
        #1485, #1515, #1585, 1970–1985, one-piece skirt, pink pindot or check dress 70.00
        #1586, 1986–1987, blue dress with striped pinafore 55.00
RED BOY 8" hp., BK, #740, 1972 (Wendy Ann) 125.00
    #0740, 1973–1975, marked "Alex." 60.00
    #440, 1976–1988 (1985–1987 white face), marked "Alexander" 55.00
RED CROSS NURSE 7" compo., 1937, 1941–1943 (Tiny Betty) 275.00
    9" compo., 1939, 1942–1943 (Little Betty) 285.00
    14" hp., 1948 only (Margaret) .... 750.00 up
RED RIDING HOOD 7" compo., 1936–1942 (Tiny Betty) 245.00
    9" compo., 1939–1940 (Little Betty) 275.00
    8" hp., SLW, #608, 1955 (Wendy Ann) 465.00
    8" hp., BKW, #382, 1962–1965, Storybook Series (Wendy Ann) 350.00
    8" hp., BK, #782, 1965–1972 .... 135.00
    8" hp., straight leg, #0782, #482, 1973–1975, marked "Alex." 60.00

14" REBECCA, 1970–1985

8" hp., straight leg, #482, 1976–1986 (1985–1987 white face), marked "Alexander" 55.00

8", #485, #463, 1987–1991 (Maggie), 1992–1993 (Wendy Ann)..55.00

RENOIR 21" compo., 1945–1946 (Wendy Ann) 2,200.00

14" hp., 1950 only (Margaret) ....875.00 up

21" hp./vinyl arms, 1961 only (Cissy) ....850.00 up

18" hp./vinyl arms, vinyl head, 1963 only (Elise) ....600.00 up

#2154, 21" hp./vinyl arms, 1965, pink gown (Jacqueline)..1,000.00

#2062, 1966, blue gown with black trim (Coco) 2,300.00

#2175, 1967, navy blue gown, red hat 675.00

#2194, #2184, 1969–1970, blue gown, full lace overdress...875.00

#2163, 1971, all yellow gown 850.00

#2190, 1972, pink gown with black jacket & trim 675.00

#2190, 1973, yellow gold gown, black ribbon 650.00

10" hp., #1175, 1968, all navy with red hat (Cissette)...450.00

#1175, 1969, pale blue gown, short jacket, stripe or dotted skirt..............................500.00

#1180, 1970, all aqua satin 450.00

RENOIR CHILD 12" plastic/vinyl, #1274, 1967 only, Portrait Children Series (Nancy Drew)..............200.00

14", #1474, 1968 only (Mary Ann) 250.00

RENOIR GIRL 14" plastic/vinyl, #1469, #1475, 1967–1968, Portrait Children Series,

white dress with red ribbon trim, (Mary Ann)...175.00

#1477, 1969–1971, pink dress, white pinafore...95.00

#1477, #1478, #1578, 1972–1986, pink multi–tiered lace gown.......................................75.00

#1572, 1986 only, pink pleated nylon dress 100.00

RENOIR GIRL WITH WATERING CAN #1577, 1985–1987, Classics & Fine Arts Series 85.00

RENOIR GIRL WITH HOOP #1574, 1986–1987, Classic & Fine Arts Series 85.00

RENOIR MOTHER 21" hp./vinyl arms, 1967 only, navy blue, red hat (Jacqueline) ....900.00 up

RHETT 12", #1380, 1981–1985, Portrait Children Series, black jacket/grey pants (Nancy Drew).........65.00

8", #401, 1989 only, Jubilee II (Wendy Ann)...95.00

8", #632, #642, 1991–1992 only, Scarlett Series, all white/blue vest 57.00

8", #642, 1993, tan pants/vest/tie with white jacket 67.00

RIDING HABIT 8", 1990 only, Americana Series (Wendy Ann) 80.00

#571, 1956 ....385.00

#373G, 1957 ....450.00 up

#541, 1958 ....385.00

#355, 1962 ....325.00

#623, 1965 ....325.00

RIDING HOOD 16" cloth/felt, 1930's 675.00

RILEY'S LITTLE ANNIE 14" plastic/vinyl, #1481, 1967 only, Literature Series (Mary Ann) 175.00

RINGBEARER 14" hp., 1951 only (Lovey Dove) ....450.00 up

RINGMASTER 8" (see C.U under Special Events/Exclusives)

RIVERBOAT QUEEN (LENA) (see M.A.D.C. under Special Events/Exclusives)

ROBIN HOOD 8", #446, 1988–1990, Storybook Series (Wendy Ann) 85.00

RODEO 8" hp., #483, 1955 only (Wendy Ann)..775.00 up

ROGERS, GINGER 14–21" compo., 1940–1945 (Wendy Ann) ....1,200.00 up

ROLLER BLADES (see Disney under Special Events/Exclusives)

ROLLER SKATING 8" hp., SL, SLW, BK, #556, 1953–1956 (Wendy Ann)..............................475.00 up

ROMANCE 21" compo., 1945–1946 (Wendy Ann) 2,200.00

ROMEO 18" compo., 1949 (Wendy Ann) ....1,400.00 up

8" hp., #474, 1955 only (Wendy Ann)...1,200.00 up

12" plastic/vinyl, #1370, 1978–1987, Portrait Children Series (Nancy Drew) 50.00

12", reintroduced 1991–1992 only, Romance Series (Nancy Drew) 92.00

ROOSEVELT, EDITH 1988, 5th set Presidents' Ladies/First Ladies Series (Louisa)....................70.00

ROOSEVELT, ELEANOR 14", 1989–1990, 6th set Presidents' Ladies/First Ladies Series (Louisa)...........100.00

ROSAMUND BRIDESMAID 15" hp., 1951 only (Margaret, Maggie)......................................500.00 up
    17–18" hp., 1951 only (Margaret, Maggie) ....600.00 up
ROSE 9" early vinyl toddler, 1953 only, pink organdy dress & bonnet....................................100.00
ROSEBUD 16–19" cloth/vinyl, 1952–1953 ....125.00
    13", 1953 only 150.00
    23–25", 1953 only 175.00
ROSEBUD (PUDDIN') 14"–20", 1986 only, white 50.00
    14", black 60.00
ROSE FAIRY 8" hp., #622, 1956 only (Wendy Ann) ....1,800.00 up
ROSETTE 10", #1115, 1987–1989, Portrette Series, pink/rose gown (Cissette) 110.00
ROSEY POSEY 14" cloth/vinyl, 1976 only 65.00
    21" cloth/vinyl, 1976 only 95.00
ROSS, BETSY 8" hp., Americana Series, 1967–1972 (Wendy Ann)
    Bend knees, #731 ....125.00
    Straight legs, #0731, #431, 1973–1975, Storybook Series, marked "Alex" 60.00
    Straight legs, #431, 1976–1987 (1985–1987 white face) 55.00
    8", #312, reintroduced 1991–1992 only, Americana Series 55.00
    #312, 1976 Bicentennial gown (stars)..100.00
ROSY 14", #1562, 1988–1990, Classic Series, all pink dress with cream lace trim (Mary Ann) 70.00
ROUND UP COWGIRL (see Disney under Special Events/Exclusives)
ROYAL EVENING 18" hp., 1953 only (Margaret) 1,600.00
ROYAL WEDDING 21" compo., 1939 only (Wendy Ann) 2,300.00
ROZY 12" plastic/vinyl, #1130, 1969 only (Janie) 400.00
RUBY (JULY) 10", #1151, 1992 only, Birthstone Collection, all red/gold (Cissette) 64.00
RUFFLES CLOWN 21", 1954 only 425.00
RUMBERA/RUMBERO 7" compo., 1938–1943 (Tiny Betty) ....each 250.00
    9" compo., 1939–1941 (Little Betty) ....each 285.00
RUMANIA 8" hp., BK, #786, 1968–1972 (Wendy Ann) 130.00
    8" straight leg, #0786, #586, 1973–1975, marked "Alex." 60.00
    8" straight leg, #586, #538, 1976–1987, marked "Alexander" 55.00
    8", #538, 1986–1987 (1986 white face) 60.00
RUMPELSTILTSKIN & MILLER'S DAUGHTER 8" & 14", #1569, 1992 only, limited to 3,000 sets 245.00
RUSSIA 8" hp., BK, #774, 1968–1972 (Wendy Ann) 125.00
    8" straight leg, #0774, 1973–1975, marked "Alex." 60.00
    8" straight leg, #574, #548, 1976–1988 (1985–1987 white face), marked "Alexander" 55.00
    8", #548, 1985–1987, white face 55.00
    8", #581, reintroduced 1991–1992 only 60.00
    9" compo, 1938–1942 (Little Betty) 300.00
RUSSIAN 7" compo., 1935–1938 (Tiny Betty) 265.00
    9" compo., 1938–1942 (Little Betty)..325.00
RUSTY 20" cloth/vinyl, 1967–1968 only..300.00

Please read "About Pricing" for additional information.

SAILOR 14" compo., 1942–1945 (Wendy Ann) 750.00
    17" compo., 1943–1944 ....900.00
    8" boy, 1990 (see U.F.D.C. under Special Events/Exclusives)
    8" boy, 1991 (see FAO Schwarz under Special Events/Exclusives)
SAILORETTE 10" hp., #1119, 1988 only, Portrette Series, red/white/blue outfit (Cissette).....................85.00
SALLY BRIDE 14" compo., 1938–1939 (Wendy Ann) ....425.00 up
    18–21" compo., 1938–1939 ....485.00 up
SALOME 14", #1412, 1984–1986, Opera Series (Mary Ann) 75.00
SAMANTHA 1989 (see FAO Schwarz under Special Events/Exclusives)
    14", #1561, 1991–1992 only, Classic Series, gold ruffled gown (Mary Ann) 170.00
SANDY MCHARE Cloth/felt, 1930's 625.00
SANTA AND MRS. CLAUS 8", mid-year issue (see Special Events/Exclusives)
SAPPHIRE (SEPTEMBER) 10", 1992 only, Birthstone Collection 64.00
SARDINIA 8", #509, 1989–1991 only (Wendy Ann)...65.00
SARGENT 14", #1576, 1984–1985, Fine Arts Series, dressed in lavender (Mary Ann)..........................75.00
SARGENT'S GIRL 14", #1579, 1986 only, Fine Arts Series, dressed in pink (Mary Ann).....................75.00
SCARECROW 8", #430, 1993, Storybook Series 62.00
SCARLETT O'HARA (pre-movie, 1937–1938)
    7" compo., 1937–1942 (Tiny Betty) 400.00
    9" compo., 1938–1941 (Little Betty) 450.00
    11", 1937–1942 (Wendy Ann) 550.00
    14–15" compo., 1941–1943 (Wendy Ann) 650.00

21" SCARLETT, 1961–1962 (CISSY)

14" SCARLETT, 1968
with gazebo made by Floyd and Gracie James.

18" compo., 1939–1946 (Wendy Ann) 1,100.00
21" compo., 1945, 1947 (Wendy Ann) 1,500.00
14–16" hp., 1950's (Margaret) 1,300.00
14–16" hp., 1950's (Maggie) 1,300.00
20" hp., 1950's (Margaret) ....1,400.00 up
18" hp./vinyl arms, 1963 only, pale blue organdy w/rosebuds, straw hat (Elise) ....900.00 up
12" hp., 1963 only, green taffeta gown and bonnet (Lissy) 1,400.00
21", 1955, 1961–1962, blue taffeta gown w/black looped braid trim (Cissy) 1,300.00
7½–8", 1953–1954, white gown w/red rosebuds, white lace hat (Wendy Ann) ....950.00 up
7½–8" hp., #485, 1955, two layer gown, white/yellow/green trim (Wendy Ann) ....850.00 up
8" hp., BKW, 1956, pink or blue floral gown ....800.00 up
8" hp., BKW, #431, 1957, white, lace and ribbon trim ....850.00 up
8" hp., BK, #760, 1963 ....700.00 up
8", BK, 1965, in white gown (Wendy Ann)...725.00 up
8", BK, #725, 1966–1972, Americana & Storybook Series, flowered gown 425.00
8", #0725, #425, 1973–1991, white gown (Wendy Ann) 65.00
   Straight leg, #425, marked "Alex." 65.00
   Straight leg, #425, #426, 1976–1986 (1985–1986 white face), marked "Alexander" 60.00
     #426, 1987 white face, blue dot gown 200.00
   Straight leg, #426, 1988–1989, flowered gown 65.00
   1986 (see M.A.D.C. under Special Events/Exclusives)
   1989 (see Child At Heart under Special Events/Exclusives)
   1989, #400, Jubilee II, green velvet/gold trim 65.00
   Straight leg, #626, 1990 only, tiny floral print 75.00
   #631, 1991 only, 3-tier white gown, curly hair 70.00
   #627, 1992 only, rose floral print, oversized bonnet...65.00
   #641, 1993, white gown with green trim...65.00
   #643, 1993, ("Honeymoon In New Orleans"), trunk with wardrobe 185.00
8" hp., 1990, M.A.D.C. Symposium (see Special Events/Exclusives)
8", 1993, mid-year issue (see Special Events/Exclusives)
21" hp./vinyl arms, #2153, 1963–1964 (became "Godey" in 1965 with blonde hair).........1,600.00 up

8" Scarlett dolls (Left to right: 1967, 1972, 1966)

21" hp./vinyl arms, 1965, #2152, green satin gown (Jacqueline) 1,300.00
    #2061, 1966, all white gown, red sash & roses (Also with plain wide lace hem;
        also inverted "V" scalloped lace hem – allow more for this gown) (Coco) 2,700.00
    #2174, 1967, green satin gown with black trim..975.00
    #2180, 1968, floral print gown with wide white hem..1,200.00 up
    #2190, 1969, red gown with white lace..800.00
    #2180, 1970, green satin, white trim on jacket..900.00
    #2292, 2295, 2296, 1975–1977, all green satin, white lace at cuffs.....................................800.00
    #2110, 1978, silk floral gown, green parasol, white lace 775.00
    #2240, 1979–1985, green velvet 450.00
    #2255, 1986 only, floral gown, green parasol, white lace 400.00
    #2247, 1987–1988, layered all over white gown...375.00
    #2253, 1989, doll has full bangs, all red gown 365.00
    #2258, 1990–1993, Scarlett Series, Scarlett Bride 400.00
    #2259, 1991–1992 only, green on white, three ruffles around skirt 300.00
    #009, porcelain, 1991 only, green velvet, gold trim 585.00
10" hp., #1174, 1968 only, lace in bonnet, green satin gown with black braid trim (Cissette) ...525.00
    #1174, 1969, green satin gown with white & gold braid 465.00
    #1181, #1180, 1970–1973, green satin gown with gold braid trim 450.00
    #1102, 1990–1991 only, Scarlett Series, floral print gown 90.00
10", #1105, 1992 only, Scarlett at Ball, all in black..100.00
10", 1993, green velvet drapes/gold trim 110.00
12", 1981–1985, green gown with braid trim (Nancy Drew) 85.00
14" plastic/vinyl, #1495, 1968, floral gown (Mary Ann) 500.00
    #1490, #7590, 1969–1986, white gown, tagged "Gone With The Wind" (Mary Ann)..............95.00
    #1590, #1591, 1987–1989, blue or green floral print on beige 95.00

14" SCARLETT, 1991; 8" BONNIE BLUE, 1993

8" SCARLETT, 1993

        #1590, 1990, Scarlett Series, tiny floral print gown 145.00
        #1595, 1991–1992 only, Scarlett Series, white ruffles, green ribbon (Louisa, Jennifer)..........147.00
    #1500, 14", 1986 only, Jubilee #1, all green velvet (Mary Ann) 185.00
    #1300, 14", 1989 only, Jubilee #2, green floral print gown (Mary Ann) 145.00
        10", #1100, burgundy & white gown (Cissette) 125.00
        8", #400, all green velvet gown (Wendy Ann) 145.00
SCARLETT, MISS 14", 1988 (see Belk's under Special Events/Exclusives)
SCASSI GOWN 21", 1990 (see FAO Schwarz under Special Events/Exclusives)
SCHOOL GIRL 7" compo., 1936–1943 (Tiny Betty) 265.00
SCOTCH 7" compo., 1936–1939 (Tiny Betty) 235.00
    9" compo., 1939–1940 (Little Betty) 265.00
    10" hp., 1962–1963 (Cissette) ....1,400.00 up
SCOTS LASS 8" hp., BKW, #396, 1963 only (Maggie Mixup, Wendy Ann) 275.00
SCOTTISH (SCOTLAND) 8" hp., BKW, #796, 1964–1965 (Wendy Ann) 175.00
    8" hp., BK, #796, 1965–1972 ....125.00
    8" straight leg, #0796-596, 1973–1975, marked "ALEX." 60.00
    8" straight leg, #596, #529, 1976–1993 only (1985–1987 white face), marked "Alexander"..........52.00
SCOUT 8", #367, 1991–1992 only, Americana Series 55.00
SEARS ROEBUCK (see Special Events/Exclusives)
SEPTEMBER 14", #1527, 1989 only, Classic Series (Mary Ann) 80.00
    10", #1152, 1992, Portrette Series, royal blue/gold flapper ....
SEVEN DWARFS Compo., 1937 only ....each 700.00 up
SHAHARAZAD 10", #1144, 1992 only, Portrette Series (Cissette) 85.00
SHEA ELF 8", 1990 (see C.U. under Special Events/Exclusives)
SHIRLEY'S DOLL HOUSE (see Special Events/Exclusives)
SICILY 8", #513, 1989–1990 (Wendy Ann) 65.00
SIMONE 21" hp./vinyl arms, 1968 only, in trunk (Jacqueline) ....1,600.00 up
SIR LAPIN HARE Cloth/felt, 1930's 650.00
SISTER BRENDA (see FAO Swartz under Special Events/Exclusives)
SITTING PRETTY 18" foam body, 1965 only 425.00
SKATER 8", 1991 (see C.U. under Special Events/Exclusives)
SKATER'S WALTZ 15"–18", 1955–1956 (Cissy) 625.00
SKATING DOLL 16", 1944–1947, (untagged "Sonja Henie") 600.00
SLEEPING BEAUTY 7–9" compo., 1941–1944 (Tiny Betty & Little Betty) 285.00
    15–16" compo., 1938–1940 (Princess Elizabeth) 450.00
    18–21" compo., 1941–1944 (Wendy Ann) 650.00
    10" hp., 1960 (Cissette)..475.00
    10", #1141, 1991–1992 only, Portrette Series, blue/white gown 95.00
    16½" hp., 1959 (Elise)..575.00
    21", 1959 only ....900.00 up
    10" hp., 1959 only, made for Disneyland, blue gown (Cissette) 465.00
    12", 1990 (see Disney under Special Events/Exclusives)
    14" plastic/vinyl, #1495, #1595, 1971–1985, Classic Series, gold gown (Mary Ann) 80.00
    14", #1596, 1986–1990, Classic Series, blue gown (Mary Ann) 80.00
SLUMBERMATE 11–12" cloth/compo., 1940's ....465.00 up
    21" compo/cloth, 1940's ....550.00 up
    13" vinyl/cloth, 1951 only ....125.00 up
SMARTY 12" plastic/vinyl, #1160, #1136, 1962–1963 ....365.00
    1963 only, "Smarty & Baby" 400.00
    1963 only, with boy "Artie" in case with wardrobe 625.00
SMEE 8", #442, 1993, Storybook Series (Peter Pan), wears glasses 62.00
SMILEY 20" cloth/vinyl, 1971 only (Happy) 265.00
SMOKEY TAIL Cloth/felt, 1930's 625.00

SNOWFLAKE (see M.A.D.C. under Special Events/Exclusives)
  10", #1167, 1993, Portrette Series, ballerina dressed in white/gold outfit (Cissette) 92.00
SNOW WHITE 13" compo., 1937–1939, painted eyes (Princess Elizabeth) 425.00
  12" compo., 1939–1940 (Princess Elizabeth)...425.00
  13" compo, 1939–1940, sleep eyes (Princess Elizabeth) 400.00
  16" compo., 1939–1942 (Princess Elizabeth)...500.00
  18" compo., 1939–1940 (Princess Elizabeth)...600.00
  14–15" hp., 1952 only (Margaret) 600.00
  18–23", 1952 only..800.00–1,000.00
  21" hp. (Margaret) 1,200.00
  14", #1455, 1967–1977, Disney Crest Color (Mary Ann) 450.00
  8" hp., 1972–1977, Disney Crest Colors (Wendy Ann) 500.00
  8", #495, 1990–1992 only, Storyland Series (Wendy Ann) 85.00
  12", 1990 (see Disney under Special Events/Exclusives)
  14" plastic/vinyl, #1455, #1555, 1970–1985, Classic Series, white gown (Mary Ann) 125.00
    #1556, #1557, 1986–1992, ecru & gold gown, red cape (Mary Ann, Louisa).........................120.00
SNOW QUEEN 10", #1130, 1991–1992 only, Portrette Series, silver/white gown (Cissette) 84.00
SO BIG 22" cloth/vinyl, 1968–1975, painted eyes 225.00
SO LITE BABY OR TODDLER 20" cloth, 1930–1940's ....325.00 up
SOLDIER 14" compo., 1943–1944 (Wendy Ann) 650.00
  17" compo., 1942–1945 (Wendy Ann) 725.00
SOUND OF MUSIC, LARGE SET, 1965–1970
  14", #1404, Louisa (Mary Ann) 300.00
  10", Friedrich (Smarty) 200.00
  14", #1403 Brigitta and #1405 Liesl (Mary Ann) ....each 225.00
  10" Marta, 10" Gretl (Smarty)..each 200.00
  17" Maria (Elise or Polly) 375.00
  Full set of 7 dolls 1,700.00
SOUND OF MUSIC, SMALL SET, 1971–1973
  12" Maria (Nancy Drew)..350.00
  8" #802 Marta, #807 Friedrich, #801 Gretl (Wendy Ann) ....each 225.00
  10" Brigitta (Cissette)..225.00
  10" Liesl (Cissette)..200.00
  10" Louisa (Cissette)..265.00
  Set of 7 dolls..1,400.00 up
SOUND OF MUSIC, DRESSED IN SAILOR SUITS & TAGGED, DATE UNKNOWN
  17" Maria (Elise or Polly) 475.00
  14" Louisa (Mary Ann)..475.00
  10" Friedrich (Smarty)...350.00
  14" Brigitta (Mary Ann)..375.00
  14" Liesl (Mary Ann)...375.00
  10" Gretl (Smarty)..350.00
  10" Marta (Smarty)..350.00
  Set of 7 dolls..2,600.00 up
  12", 1965, in sailor suit (Lissy)...500.00
SOUND OF MUSIC All in same oufit: red skirt, white attached blouse,
  black vest that ties in front with gold cord ....each 400.00–600.00
SOUND OF MUSIC, REINTRODUCED 1992
  8", #390, #391, 1992–1993, Gretl and Kurt (boy in sailor suit) ....each 60.00
  8", #390, #392, 1992–1993, Brigitta 55.00
  8", #394, 1993, Friedrich dressed in green/white playsuit...60.00
  8", #393, 1993, Marta in sailor dress 60.00
  10", 1992–1993, Maria (Cissette) 85.00

12", 1992 only, Maria Bride (Nancy Drew) 135.00

10", "Maria At Abbey," dressed in nun's outfit (Cissette) 75.00

SOUTH AMERICAN 7" compo., 1938–1943 (Tiny Betty)...265.00

9" compo., 1939–1941 (Little Betty) 285.00

SOUTHERN BELLE OR GIRL 8" hp., #370, 1954 (Wendy Ann) ....1,300.00 up

8" hp., #408, 1955 (Wendy Ann)...865.00

8" hp., #437, #410, 1956, pink or blue/white stripe gown (Wendy Ann) 925.00

8" hp., #385, 1963 only (Wendy Ann)..500.00

12" hp., 1963 only (Lissy)...1,200.00

21" hp./vinyl arms., #2155, 1965, blue gown with wide pleated hem (Jacqueline)...................1,200.00

#2170, 1967, white gown with green ribbon trim 900.00

#2220, 1979–1981, pink with blue ribbon trim ....775.00 up

10" hp., #1170, 1968, white gown with green ribbon through 3 rows of lace (Cissette)............475.00

1969, white gown with 4 rows of lace, pink sash 450.00

#1185, 1970, white gown with red ribbon sash...450.00

#1185 (#1184 in 1973) 1971–1973, white gown with green ribbon sash 425.00

10" (see My Doll House under Special Events/Exclusives)

SOUTHERN GIRL 11–14" compo., 1940–1943 (Wendy Ann) 500.00

17–21" compo., 1940–1943 (Wendy Ann)...700.00–750.00

SOUTHERN SYMPOSIUM (see M.A.D.C. under Special Events/Exclusives)

SPANISH 7–8" compo., 1935–1939 (Tiny Betty) 265.00

9" compo., 1936–1940 (Litte Betty)...285.00

SPANISH BOY 8" hp., BK & BKW, #779, 1964–1968 (Wendy Ann) 365.00

SPANISH GIRL 8" hp., BKW, #795, #395, 1962–1965, three-tiered skirt (Wendy Ann) 175.00

8" hp., BK, #795, 1965–1972, three-tiered skirt 135.00

8" straight leg, #0795, #595, 1973–1975, three-tiered skirt, marked "ALEX." 85.00

8" straight leg, #595, 1976–1982, three-tiered skirt, marked "Alexander".............................65.00

8" straight leg, #595, 1983–1985, two-tiered skirt (1985 white face) 55.00

8" straight leg, #541, 1986–1990, white with red polka dots (1986–1987 white face) 60.00

8" straight leg, #541, 1990–1992, all red tiered skirt..55.00

SPANISH MATADOR 8", #530, 1992–1993 (Wendy Ann) 58.00

SPECIAL EVENTS/EXCLUSIVES Shops and organizations are listed alphabetically.

ABC UNLIMITED PRODUCTIONS

WENDY LEARNS HER ABC'S 8", 1993, wears blue jumber and beret, ABC blocks on skirt,

wooden block stand 90.00

BELKS DEPARTMENT STORES

MISS SCARLETT 14", 1988 ....120.00

RACHEL/RACHAEL 8", 1988, lavender gown ....each 80.00

NANCY JEAN 8", 1990, yellow/brown outfit 65.00

FANNIE ELIZABETH 8", 1991, limited to 3,000, floral dress with pinafore 70.00

ANNABELLE AT CHRISTMAS 8", 1992, limited to 3,000, plaid dress, holds Christmas cards...........75.00

CAROLINE 8", 1993 ....80.00

CELIA'S DOLLS

DAVID, THE LITTLE RABBI 8", 1991–1992 ....85.00

CHILD AT HEART

SCARLETT WITH TRUNK AND WARDROBE 8", 1989 (trunk and wardrobe added) 265.00

EASTER BUNNY 8", 1990, limit: 3,000 (1,500 blondes, 750 brunettes, 750 redheads) 325.00

MY LITTLE SWEETHEART 8", limit: 4,500 (1,000 blondes, 1,000 brunettes w/blue eyes,

1,000 brunettes w/green eyes, 1,000 redheads w/green eyes, 500 blacks) 85.00

TRICK AND TREAT 8", 1993, sold in sets only

(400 sets with red haired/green eyed "Trick" and black "Treat;"

1,200 sets with red haired/green eyed "Trick" and brunette/brown eyed "Treat;"

1,400 blonde/blue eyed "Trick" and red haired/brown eyed "Treat.") ....set 160.00

CHRISTMAS SHOPPE
  BOY & GIRL IN ALPINE   8" twins, 1992, in alpine outfits, limit: 2,000 sets .... pair 200.00
COLLECTOR UNITED (C.U.)
  YUGOSLAVIA   8", 1987, F.A.D., limit: 625 .... 130.00
  TIPPI BALLERINA   8", 1988, limit: 800 .... 350.00
  MISS LEAH   8", 1989, limit: 1,000 .... 200.00
  BRIDE   8", 1989, F.A.D., limit: 500 (Betsy Brooks) 95.00
  SHEA ELF   8", 1990, limit: 1000 .... 185.00
  WITCH/HALLOWEEN   8", 1990, F.A.D., limit: 500 (Little Jumping Joan) 125.00
  NASHVILLE SKATER #1, (WINTER WONDERLAND)   8", 1991, F.A.D., limit: 500 (Black Forest) 90.00
  NASHVILLE SKIER #2,   8", 1992, F.A.D, limit: 200 (Tommy Tittlemouse) 90.00
  NASHVILLE #3, FIRST COMES LOVE BRIDE   8", 1993, limit: 200 .... 85.00
  CAMEO LADY   10", 1991, doll shop exclusive, limit: 3,000, white/black trim 125.00
  RINGMASTER   8", 1991, F.A.D., limit: 1,000 (Lion Tamer) 165.00
  CAMELOT   8", 1991, F.A.D. (Columbia, SC) (Maid Marion) 125.00
  FAITH   8", 1992, limit: 900 .... 250.00
  HOPE   8", 1993, limit: 900, blue dress (1910 style) 165.00
  OKTOBERFEST   8", 1992, F.A.D. (Austria) 85.00
  LE PETITE BOUDOIR   10", 1993, doll shop exclusive, F.A.D. (Cissette) 90.00

**QUEEN OF HEARTS (Disneyworld Special)
shown with hedgehog and flamingo.**

Left: 8" Disneyworld Special, luncheon doll of 1984.

DISNEY, WALT

 DISNEYWORLD AUCTION 21", one of kind dolls

  CHRISTINE (PHANTOM OF THE OPERA) #1, 1990 blue/white outfit with white mask
  (Jacqueline) ....6,500.00 up

  QUEEN ISABELLA #2, 1991, green/gold gown, long red hair (Jacqueline)...................6,500.00 up

  IT'S A GIRL #3, 1992, comes with 8" baby in carriage (Cissy, Baby Genuis) ....6,500.00 up

  EMPEROR AND NIGHTINGALE #4, 1992, 8" bird (23" Emperor bear by Gund)..............6,500.00 up

 CINDERELLA 10", 1989, #1 Annual Showcase of Dolls, blue satin gown, limit: 250 ....700.00

 SNOW WHITE 12", 1990, #2 Annual Showcase of Dolls, limit: 750 (Nancy Drew) 250.00

 ALICE IN WONDERLAND/WHITE RABBIT 10", 1991, #3 Annual Showcase of Dolls......................350.00

 QUEEN OF HEARTS 10", 1992, #4 Annual Showcase of Dolls, limit: 500 ....350.00

 BOBBY SOXER 8", 1990–1991 ....125.00

 SLEEPING BEAUTY 12", 1990–1991 (Nancy Drew) 225.00

 MOUSEKETEER 8", 1991 ....95.00

 ROUND UP COWGIRL 8", 1992, blue/white outfit..90.00

 ROLLER BLADES 8", 1992, "Throughly Modern Wendy" 95.00

 MONIQUE 8", 1993, made for Disneyland, limit: 250, lavendar with lace trim ....650.00 up

 SNOW WHITE 10", 1993, Crest Colors 150.00

 DRUCILLA 14", 1992, F.A.D. (Queen), Disneyland convention lottery, limit: 268 ....265.00

 ANASTASIA 14", 1993, made for Disneyland, limit: 386 ....300.00

DOLL FINDERS

 FANTASY 8", 1990, limit: 350 ....225.00

DOLLS 'N BEARLAND

 PANDORA 8", 1991, limit: 3,600 (950 brunette, 950 redheads, 1,700 blondes)..........................85.00

8" BO PEEP, 1987
Special for Dolly Dears; sheep made by R. Dakin

DOLLY DEARS

    BO PEEP 1987, holds staff, black sheep wears man's hat, white sheep wears girl's hat (Sheep made exclusive by Dakin) 275.00

    SUSANNA CLOGGER 8", 1992, has freckles, limit: 400 (Maggie) 300.00

    JACK BE NIMBLE 8", 1993, F.A.D., limit: 288 ....185.00

    PRINCESS AND THE PEA 8", 1993 ....95.00

ENCHANTED DOLL HOUSE

    RICK-RACK ON PINAFORE 8", 1980 ....265.00

    EYELET PINAFORE 8", 1981 ....275.00

    25TH ANNIVERSARY 10", 1988, long gown 165.00

    BLUE BALLERINA 8", 1985, F.A.D, blonde or brunette doll in trunk with extra clothes 175.00

    VERMONT MAIDEN 8", 1990–1992, official Vermont bicentennial doll, limit: 3,600 (800 blondes, 2,800 brunettes) 125.00

    FARMER'S DAUGHTER 8", 1991, limit: 4,000 (1,000 blondes, 1,500 redheads, 1,500 brunettes)..125.00

    FARMER'S DAUGHTER 8", 1992, "Goes To Town" (Cape and basket added), limit: 1,600 ....75.00

FAO SCHWARZ

    SAMANTHA 14", 1989, white with black dots (Mary Ann) 125.00

    DAVID AND DIANE 8", 1989, in red, white, and demin, with wooden wagon ....set 160.00

    BROOKE 14", 1989 (Mary Ann) 90.00

    ME & MY SCASSI 21", 1990, all in red (Cissy) 300.00

    SAILOR 8", 1991 ....75.00

    CARNVALE DOLL 14", 1992 (Samatha) 145.00

    BEDDY-BYE BROOKE 14", 1991–1992 ....125.00

        BEDDY-BYE BRENDA (BROOKE'S SISTER) 8", 1992, sold only in set ....set 240.00

    WENDY SHOPS FAO 8", 1993, red/white outfit, carries FAO Schwarz shopping bag 78.00

FIRST MODERN DOLL CLUB

    AUTUMN IN N.Y. 10", 1991, F.A.D., red skirt, fur trim cape/hat/muff/skates, limit: 260 ....200.00

HORCHOW

    PAMELA PLAYS DRESS UP 12", 1993, in trunk with wardrobe, limit: 1,250 (Lissy) 265.00

I. MAGNIN

    CHEERLEADER 8", 1990, F.A.D. 100.00

    MISS MAGNIN 10", 1991–1993, limit: 2,500 (Cissette) 150.00

    LITTLE MISS MAGNIN 8", 1992, with tea set and teddy bear, limit: 3,600 ....100.00

    BON VOYAGE MISS MAGNIN 10", 1993, navy/white gloves, has steamer trunk, limit: 2,500 ....115.00

    BON VOYAGE LITTLE MISS MAGNIN 8", sailor dress, carries teddy bear/suitcase, limit: 3,500 ....95.00

IMAGINARIUM SHOP

    LITTLE HUGGUMS 12", 1991, special outfits, bald or wigged 60.00

MADAME ALEXANDER DOLL CLUB (M.A.D.C. CONVENTION DOLLS)

    FAIRY OUTFIT 1983, for 8" non-Alexander 300.00

    BALLERINA 8", 1984, F.A.D. 225.00

    HAPPY BIRTHDAY 8", 1985, F.A.D. 325.00

    SCARLETT 8", 1986, F.A.D., red instead of green ribbon, limit: 700 ....325.00

    COWBOY 8", 1987 ....475.00

    FLAPPER 10", 1988, F.A.D., black outfit instead of red 150.00

    BRIAR ROSE 8", 1989, uses Cissette head 300.00

    RIVERBOAT QUEEN (LENA) 8", 1990 ....325.00

    QUEEN CHARLOTTE 10", 1991, blue/gold outfit, limit: under 900 ....325.00

    PROM QUEEN (MEMORIES) 8", 1992, limit: 1,100 ....300.00

    DIAMOND LIL (DAYS GONE BY) 10", 1993, black gown, limit: 876 ....350.00

M.A.D.C. DOLLS, EXCLUSIVES (AVAILABLE TO CLUB MEMBERS ONLY)

    WENDY 8", 1989, in pink and blue 165.00

    POLLY PIGTAILS 8", 1990 (Maggie Mixup) 150.00

    MISS LIBERTY 10", 1991–1992, red/white/blue gown (Cissette) 125.00

Miss Godey 8", 1992 ....165.00
M.A.D.C. Symposium/Premier
    Pre-Doll Specials (M.A.D.C. Symposium)
    Disneyworld 1984–1985 (1984 - Paperdoll) 60.00
    Wendy Goes To Disneyworld #1 Sunshine Symposium, 1986, limit: 100,
        navy dress with polka dots, Mickey Mouse hat, pennent (costume by Dorothy Starling) 95.00
    Snowflake Symposium 1st Illinois, 1986, tagged orange taffeta/lace dress, metal pail and orange,
        limit: 200 ....95.00
        2nd Illinois, 1987, tagged, little girl cotton print dress (costume by Mary Voigt) 85.00
        3rd Illinois, 1988, tagged, gold/white print dress, gold bodice (created by Pamela Martenec) 85.00
        4th Illinois, 1989, tagged, red velvet ice skating costume (created by Joan Dixan) 75.00
        5th Illinois, 1990, bride by Linda Bridal Gown (also Michelau Scarlett could be purchased) 60.00
    Scarlett 8", 1990, #6, F.A.D. (white medallion – Snowflake Symposium;
        red medallion – Premier Southern Symposium) 185.00
        (Medallions: Midwest – rose; Southwest – peach; Southeast – blue; Northeast – lavender;
        West Coast – yellow; Northwest – green.)
    Springtime 8", 1991, #7, floral dress, scalloped pinafore, straw hat, limit: 1,600 ....200.00
    Wintertime 8", 1992, #8, all white, fur trim and hat (six locations), limit: 1,600 ....200.00
    Homecoming 8", 1993, 8th carcoat with red trim (eight location), limit: 2,000 ....200.00
Madame Alexander Doll Company
    Melody & Friends 25", limit: 1,000, designed and made by Hildegard Gunzel,
        first anniversary dolls ....900.00 up
    Courtney & Friends 25" & 8" boy and girl, second anniversary, by Gunzel ....set 850.00

Wendy Visits World Fair, 1993

S

MADAME ALEXANDER DOLL COMPANY MID-YEAR SPECIALS
WELCOME HOME 8", 1991, black or white, boy or girl, Desert Storm soldier 80.00
WENDY LOVES BEING LOVED 8", 1992, doll and wardrobe..165.00
QUEEN ELIZABETH II 8", 1992, 40th anniversary doll..145.00
MADAME 8", 1993, same as 21" doll, pink gown...115.00
SCARLETT 8", 1993, yellow dress 75.00
SANTA OR MRS. CLAUS 8" ....each 62.00–75.00
MARSHALL FIELDS
AVRIL, JANE 10", 1989, red/black can-can outfit (Cissette) 175.00
MADAME BUTTERFLY 10", 1990 ....95.00
METROPLEX DOLL CLUB
SPRING BREAK 8", 1992, 2-piece halter/wrap skirt outfit, limit: 400......................................350.00
MY DOLL HOUSE
SOUTHERN BELLE 10", 1989, F.A.D., all pink gown with parasol and picture hat 125.00
QUEEN ELIZABETH I 10", 1990...150.00
EMPRESS ELIZABETH OF AUSTRIA 10", 1991, white/gold trim (Cissette) 150.00
NEW ENGLAND COLLECTOR SOCIETY
NOEL 12", 1989–1991, porcelain Christmas doll, limit: 5,000 ....250.00
JOY 12", 1991, porcelain Christmas doll, limit: 5,000 ....250.00
NEIMAN-MARCUS
DOLL WITH FOUR OUTFITS IN TRUNK 8", 1990 ....200.00
WENDY LOVES STORYLAND 8", 1993, trunk and wardrobe 225.00
SAKS FIFTH AVENUE
CAROL 8", 1993 ....75.00
SEARS-ROEBUCK
LITTLE WOMEN 1990, set of six 12" dolls (Nancy Drew) ....set 375.00
SHIRLEY'S DOLL HOUSE
ANGEL FACE 8", 1990 (Maggie Mixup) 100.00
WINTER SPORTS 8", 1991, F.A.D. (Tommy Snooks) 80.00
WENDY VISITS WORLD FAIR 1993, 100th anniversary Chicago World's Fair, limit: 3,600..........85.00
WINTER ANGEL Has cape with hood, wings, and holds golden horn, exclusive: 1,000 ....87.00
SHRINER'S 1ST LADIES LUNCHEON 8" boy, 1993, wears fez, jeans, shirt, vest/Texas star on back.350.00 up
SPIEGEL'S
BETH 10", 1990, 1860's women 150.00
CHRISTMAS TREE TOPPER (Also called MERRY ANGEL) 8", 1991 ....185.00
JOY NOEL 8", 1992, tree topper angel, white satin/net with gold dots, gold/lace halo & skirt ..125.00
MARDI GRAS 10", 1992, elaborate costume of purple/gold/royal blue 125.00
U.F.D.C. – UNITED FEDERATION OF DOLL CLUBS
SAILOR BOY 8", limit: 250 ....700.00
MISS UNITY 10", 1991 ....400.00
LITTLE EMPEROR 8", 1992, limit: 400 ....450.00
TURN OF THE CENTURY BATHING BEAUTY 10", 1992, UFDC Region Nine Conference,
   F.A.D. (Gibson Girl), old fashion bathing suit, beach bag, and umbrella 250.00
SAILOR 12", 1993 (Lissy) 100.00
SPECIAL GIRL 23–24" cloth/compo., 1942–1946 ....500.00 up
SPIEGEL'S (see Special Events/Exclusives)
SPRING 14", 1993, Changing Seasons Series, doll and four extra outfits.................................155.00
SPRINGTIME 8", M.A.D.C. (see Special Events/Exclusives)
SPRING BREAK Metroplex Doll Club (see Special Events/Exclusives)
STILTS 8", #320, 1992–1993, clown on stilts..60.00
STORY PRINCESS 15–18" hp., 1954–1956 (Margaret, Cissy, Binnie)...750.00
   8" hp., #892, 1956 only (Wendy Ann)..1,300.00

STUFFY (BOY) Hp., 1952–1953 (Margaret) 850.00
SUELLEN 14–17" compo., 1937–1938 (Wendy Ann) ....950.00 up
   12", 1990 only, yellow multi-tiered skirt, Scarlett Series (Nancy Drew) 75.00
SUGAR DARLIN' 14–18" cloth/vinyl, 1964 only 100.00
   24", 1964 only 150.00
   Lively, 14", 18", 24", 1964 only, knob makes head & limbs move...............................125.00–165.00
SUGAR PLUM FAIRIE 10", #1147, 1992–1993 only, Portrette Series, lavendar ballerina 95.00
SUGAR TEARS 12" vinyl baby, 1964 only. (Honey Bea) 100.00
SULKY SUE 8", #445, 1988–1990, marked "Alexander" (Wendy Ann) 90.00
SUMMER 14", 1993, Changing Seasons Series, doll and four outfits 145.00
SUNBEAM 11", 16", 19", 1951 only, newborn infant 75.00–90.00
SUNBONNET SUE 9" compo., 1937–1940 (Little Betty) 275.00
SUNFLOWER CLOWN 40" all cloth, 1951 only, flower eyes ....800.00 up
SUPERIOR QUINTS 8" compo. (made in Canada) ....each 105.00   set 600.00
SUSANNA CLOGGERS 8" (see Dolly Dears under Special Events/Exclusives)
SUSIE Q Cloth, 1940–1942 ....650.00
SUZY 12" plastic/vinyl, 1970 only (Janie) 375.00
SWEDEN (SWISS) 8 hp., BKW, #392, #792, 1961–1965 (Wendy Ann) 175.00
   8" hp., BK, #792, 1965–1972 ....125.00
   8" straight leg, #0792, #592, 1973–1975, marked "Alex." 60.00
   8" straight leg, #592, #539, #521, 1976–1989, marked "Alexander" 55.00
   8", 1986, white face 55.00
   8", #580, reintroduced 1991 only...55.00
   BKW with Maggie Mixup face 265.00
SWEDISH 7" compo., 1936–1940 (Tiny Betty)..245.00
   9" compo., 1937–1941 (Little Betty) 275.00
SWEET BABY 18½"–20" cloth/latex, 1948 only 40.00–50.00
SWEET BABY 14", 1983–1984, (Sweet Tears)..60.00
   14", reissued 1987, 1987–1993 (1991 has no bottle) (Sweet Tears)...................................75.00
   14", 1990–1992 only (1991 has bottle), in carrycase......................................95.00–125.00
   14", reintroduced 1993, pink stripe jumper or dress 85.00
SWEET SIXTEEN 14", #1554, 1991–1992 only, Classic Series (Louisa) 125.00
SWEET TEARS 9" vinyl, 1965–1974 ....45.00
   Discontinued 1973, with layette in box...135.00
   14", 1967–1974, in trunk/trousseau ....250.00 up
   14", 1965–1974, in window box ....175.00 up
   14", 1979, with layette...150.00
   14", 1965–1982...60.00
   16", 1965–1971...85.00
SWEET VIOLET 18" hp., 1951–1954 (Cissy) ....725.00 up
SWEETIE BABY 22", 1962 only 125.00
SWEETIE WALKER 23", 1962 only ....250.00 up
SWISS 7" compo., 1936 (Tiny Betty) 245.00
   9" compo., 1935–1938 (Little Betty) 265.00
   10" hp., 1962–1963 (Cissette)...1,200.00
SWITZERLAND/SWISS 8" hp., BKW, #394, #794, 1961–1965 ....175.00
   8" hp., BK, #794, 1965–1972 ....125.00
   8" hp., straight leg, #0794, #594, 1973–1975, marked "Alex." 60.00
   8" hp., straight leg, #594, #540, #518, 1976–1989, marked "Alexander" 55.00
   8", #546, 1986, white face 55.00
   #518, 1988–1990, costume change 60.00
   8" BKW (Maggie Mixup face) 275.00
SYLVESTER THE JESTER 14", #1563, 1992–1993 (Mary Ann)...105.00
SYMPOSIUM M.A.D.C. (see Special Events/Exclusives)

Please read "About Pricing" for additional information.

Taft, Helen   1988, 5th set Presidents' Ladies/First Ladies Series (Louisa) 70.00
Teeny Twinkle   1946 only, cloth with flirty eyes, ...550.00
Tennis   8" hp., BKW, #415, #632 (Wendy Ann) 345.00
Texas   8", #313, 1991 only, Americana...60.00
Thailand   8" hp., BK, #767, 1966–1972 (Wendy Ann) 135.00
    8" straight leg, #0767, #567, 1973–1975, marked "Alex." 60.00
    8" straight leg, #567, 1976–1989 (1985–1987 white face), marked "Alexander"........55.00
Thomas, Marlo   17" plastic/vinyl, 1967 only (Polly) ....550.00 up
Three Little Pigs & Wolf   Compo., 1938–1939..each 600.00 up
Thumbelina & Her Lady   8" & 21" porcelain, 1992–1993, limit: 2,500 sets.....................550.00
Tierney, Gene   14–17" compo., 1945 (Wendy Ann) 1,400.00
Tibet   8" hp., #534, 1993 ....57.00
Tiger Lily   8", #469, 1992–1993, Storybook Series (Peter Pan) (Wendy Ann) 55.00
Timmy Toddler   23" plastic/vinyl, 1960–1961 ....165.00
    30", 1960 only 200.00
Tinker Bell   11" hp., #1110, 1969 only, Peter Pan Series (Cissette) ....600.00 up
Tinkerbelle   8" hp., 1993, Storyland Series, has magic wand 65.00

10" Tinker Bell, 1969

Tin Woodsman   8", #432, 1993, Storybook Series 62.00
Tiny Betty   7" compo., 1935–1942 ....245.00
Tiny Tim   7" compo., 1934–1937 (Tiny Betty) 275.00
    14" compo., 1938–1940 (Wendy Ann) 575.00
    Cloth, early 1930's 675.00
Tippi   8", 1988 (see C.U. under Special Events/Exclusives)
Tippy Toe   16" cloth, 1940's...625.00
Tom Sawyer   8" hp., #491, 1989–1990, Storybook Series (Maggie Mixup)...........................85.00
Tommy   12" hp., 1962 only (Lissy)..1,100.00
    15" hp., 1950–1952 (Little Men) (Margaret, Maggie) 850.00

TOMMY BANGS Hp., 1952 only (Maggie) ....800.00 up
    Disney marionettes ....275.00 up
TOPSY-TURVY Compo. with Tiny Betty heads, 1935 only 200.00
    With Dionne Quint head, 1936 only 300.00
TOULOUSE-LAUTREC 21", #2250, 1986–1987 only, black/pink outfit 265.00
TOY SOLDIER 8", #481, 1993, Storybook Series, white face, red dots on cheeks 62.00
TRAPEZE ARTIST 10", #1133, 1990–1991, Portrette Series (Cissette) 95.00
TREE TOPPER 8" (doll only), #850, 1992, red/gold dress 85.00
    8" (doll only), #852, 1992–1993, "Angel Lace" with multi-laced skirt 75.00
    8" (doll only), #853, 1993, red velvet dress...90.00
    8" (doll only), #854, 1993, pink victorian 80.00
TREENA BALLERINA 15" hp., 1952 only (Margaret)...750.00 up
    18–21", 1952 only ....900.00 up
TRUMAN, BESS 14", 1989–1990, 6th set First Ladies/Presidents' Ladies Series (Mary Ann) 100.00
TUNISIA 8", #514, 1989 only, marked "Alexander" (Wendy Ann) 80.00
TURKEY 8" hp., BK, #787, 1968–1972 (Wendy Ann)..125.00
    8" straight leg, #0787, #587, 1973–1975, marked "Alex." 60.00
    8" straight leg, #587, 1976–1986 (1985–1986 white face), marked "Alexander" 55.00
TWEEDLEDUM & TWEEDLEDEE 14" cloth, 1930–1931 ....each 700.00
20'S TRAVELER 10", #1139, 1991–1992 only, Portrette Series, M.A. signature logo on box (Cissette) 74.00
    25th anniversary, 1982, Enchanted Doll House (see Special Events/Exclusives)
TYLER, JULIA 1979–1981, 2nd set Presidents' Ladies/First Ladies Series (Martha) 90.00
TYROLEAN BOY & GIRL* 8" hp., BKW,
    (girl - #398, #798; boy - #399, #799), 1962–1965 (Wendy Ann)..each 165.00
    8" hp., BK, (girl - #798; boy - #799), 1965–1972 ....each 145.00
    8" straight leg, (girl - #0798; boy - #0799), 1973, marked "ALEX." ....each 60.00
    8" BKW, (Maggie Mixup) ....each 200.00

* *Became* AUSTRIA *in 1974.*

Please read "About Pricing" for additional information.

U.F.D.C. Sailor Boy   1990 (see Special Events/Exclusives)
U.S.A.   8" hp., #536, 1993 ....54.00
United States   8" hp., #559, straight leg, 1974–1975, marked "Alex." 55.00
   Straight leg, #559, 1976–1987 (1985–1987 white face), marked "Alexander" 55.00
   #559, #516, 1988–1992 (Maggie face) 50.00
Union Officer   12", #634, 1990–1991, Scarlett Series (Nancy Drew) 80.00
   8", #634, 1991 only, Scarlett Series 85.00
Van Buren, Angelica   1979–1981, 2nd set Presidents' Ladies/First Ladies Series (Louisa) 90.00
Vermont Maid   Enchanted Doll House (see Special Events/Exclusives)
Victoria   21" compo., 1939, 1941 (Wendy Ann) ....2,200.00 up
   21" compo., 1945–1946 (Flavia) ....2,300.00 up
   20" hp., 1954 only, Me & My Shadow Series (Cissy) 1,600.00
   14" hp., 1950–1951 (Margaret) 1,100.00
   18" hp., 1954 only, Me & My Shadow Series, slate blue gown (Margaret) 1,600.00
   8" hp., #0030C, 1954 only, matches 18" doll (Wendy Ann) ....1,200.00 up
   14" baby, 1975–1988, 1990–1993 ....105.00
   18" baby, 1966 only 85.00
   18" reintroduced, 1991–1993 ....85.00
   20" baby, 1967–1989 ....40.00–55.00
   20" 1986 only, in dress/jacket/bonnet 95.00
Victorian   18" hp., 1953 only, blue taffeta/black velvet gown, Glamour Girl Series (Margaret) 1,600.00
Victorian Bride   10", #1148, #1118, 1992 only, Portrette Series 105.00
Victorian Skater   10", #1155, 1993, Portrette Series, red/gold/black outfit (Cissette) 105.00
Vietnam   8" hp., #788, 1968–1969 (Wendy Ann)..360.00
   #788, 1968–1969 (Maggie Mixup) 350.00
   8", #505, reintroduced in 1990–1991, (Maggie)..60.00
Violet (see "Sweet Violet")
Violetta   10", #1116, 1987–1988, all deep blue (Cissette) 85.00

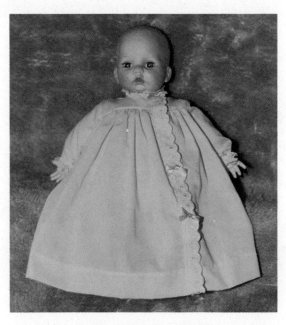

14" Victoria, 1975

Please read "About Pricing" for additional information.

W.A.A.C. (ARMY) 14" compo., 1943–1944 (Wendy Ann) ....650.00 up
W.A.A.F. (AIR FORCE) 14" compo., 1943–1944 (Wendy Ann) ....650.00 up
W.A.V.E. (NAVY) 14" compo., 1943–1944 (Wendy Ann) ....650.00 up
WALTZING 8" hp., #476, 1955 only (Wendy Ann) ....575.00 up
WASHINGTON, MARTHA 1976–1978, 1st set Presidents' Ladies/First Ladies Series (Martha) 200.00
WELCOME HOME–DESERT STORM 8", 1991 only, mid-year introduction,
    boy or girl soldier, black or white 75.00
WENDY "LOVES BEING LOVED" 8", 1992 only, mid-year introduction, doll and wardrobe 105.00
    BEING JUST LIKE MOMMY 8", #801, 1993, has baby carriage 82.00
    THE COUNTRY FAIR 8", #802, 1993, has cow 60.00
    LOVE SUMMER 8", #805, 1993, boxed doll and wardrobe 85.00
WENDY LEARNS HER ABC'S (see ABC Unlimited under Special Events/Exclusives)
WENDY VISITS WORLD FAIR (see Shirley's Doll House under Special Events/Exclusvies)
WENDY (FROM PETER PAN) 15" hp., 1953 only (Margaret) ....550.00 up
    14" plastic/vinyl, #1415, 1969 only (Mary Ann) 325.00
    8", #466, 1991–1993, Storyland Series, pom-poms on slippers (Peter Pan) 55.00

QUEEN and WENDY LOVES BEING LOVED
Madame Alexander Doll Company mid-year issues, 1992

WENDY ANGEL 8" hp., #404, 1954 (Wendy Ann) ....985.00 up
WENDY ANN 11–15" compo., 1935–1948 ....450.00
    9" compo., 1936–1940, painted eyes 325.00
    14", 1938–1939, in riding habit..500.00
    14", any year, swivel waist...450.00
    17–21" compo., 1938–1944 ....600.00–800.00
    14½–17" hp., 1948–1949...725.00–875.00
    16–22" hp., 1948–1950 ....775.00–925.00
    20" hp., 1956 (Cissy)..600.00
    23–25" hp., 1949 ....800.00
    8", 1989, first M.A.D.C. doll (see Special Events/Exclusives)
WENDY BRIDE 14–22" compo., 1944–1945 (Wendy Ann) 300.00–500.00
    15–18" hp., 1951 (Margaret) 300.00–425.00
    20" hp., 1956 (Cissy)..475.00
    23" hp., 1951 (Margaret) 550.00
    8" hp., SLW, #475, 1955 (Wendy Ann) 365.00
WITCH 8", #322, 1992–1993, Americana Series 55.00
WITCH/HALLOWEEN (see C.U. under Special Events/Exclusives)
WHITE RABBIT Cloth/felt, 1940's 625.00
WILSON, EDITH 1988, 5th set Presidents' Ladies/First Ladies Series (Mary Ann)...............110.00
WILSON, ELLEN 1988, 5th set Presidents' Ladies/First Ladies Series (Louisa) 70.00
WINNIE WALKER 15" hp., 1953 only (Cissy) 165.00
    18–23"...250.00–350.00
    1953–1954, in trunk/trousseau ....800.00 up
WINTER 14", 1993, Changing Seasons Series, doll and four outfits.......................................155.00
WINTER SPORTS 1991 (see Shirley's Doll House under Special Events/Exclusives)
WINTER WONDERLAND 1991 (see C.U. under Special Events/Exclusives)
WINTERTIME (see M.A.D.C. under Special Events/Exclusives)
WITCH 8", #322, 1992–1993, Americana Series 55.00
WITHERS, JANE 12–13½" compo., 1937, has closed mouth ....975.00 up
    15–17", 1937–1939 ....1,300.00
    17" cloth body, 1939 ....1,400.00
    18–19", 1937–1939...1,400.00
    19–20", closed mouth 1,500.00
    20–21", 1937 ....1,600.00
1860's WOMEN 10" hp., 1990 (see Spiegel's under Special Events/Exclusives)
WYNKIN (see "Dutch Lullaby")
YOLANDA 12", 1965 only (Brenda Starr)...325.00
YUGOSLAVIA 8" hp., BK, #789, 1968–1972 (Wendy Ann) 125.00
    8" straight leg, #0789, #589, 1973–1975, marked "Alex." 60.00
    8" straight leg, #589, 1976–1986 (1985–1986 white face), marked "Alexander"...........50.00
    8", 1987 (see C.U. under Special Events/Exclusives)
ZORINA BALLERINA 17" compo., 1937–1938 (Wendy Ann) 1,200.00

Schroeder's
ANTIQUES
Price Guide

. . . is the #1 best-selling antiques & collectibles value guide on the market today, and here's why . . .

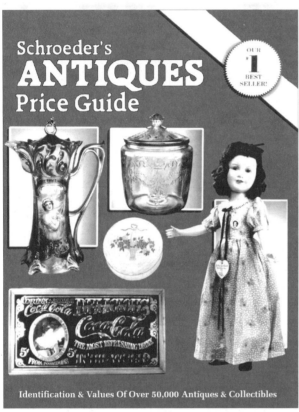

8½ x 11, 608 Pages, $12.95

COLLECTOR BOOKS
A Division of Schroeder Publishing Co., Inc.